CHILDREN JUST LIKE ME

CELEBRATION!

Written by ANABEL KINDERSLEY
Photographed by BARNABAS KINDERSLEY

DORLING KINDERSLEY
London • New York • Moscow • Sydney

Contents

A DORLING KINDERSLEY BOOK

Project Editor Fiona Robertson **Project Art Editor** Rebecca Johns
Editorial Adviser Shalini Dewan, Chief of Editorial and Publications, UNICEF
Production Charlotte Traill **Picture Research** Mollie Gillard
Managing Editor Ann Kramer **Managing Art Editor** Peter Bailey
Editorial Director Sophie Mitchell **Art Director** Miranda Kennedy

First published in Great Britain in 1997 by Dorling Kindersley Limited,
9 Henrietta Street, London WC2E 8PS
Copyright © 1997 Dorling Kindersley Limited, London

Visit us on the World Wide Web at http://www.dk.com

Find this symbol to check out the *Children Just Like Me* e-pal club
and talk to other children around the world and to the authors of this book.

Details of the royalties payable to UNICEF can be obtained by
writing to the publisher, Dorling Kindersley Limited at the above address.

A CIP catalogue record for this book is available from the British Library.

ISBN 0 7513 5650 6

Colour reproduction by Colourscan, Singapore and Mullis Morgan, UK
Printed and bound in Italy by New Interlitho Italia

PARTIES, FESTIVALS, CELEBRATIONS are often the bright stars in our memories of our early years. A birthday or some special event in the life of our family, our school, our community, or the country where we live are eagerly awaited. What we celebrate may differ, but the excitement communicated in the pages of this book shows how similar we are.

Celebration! – a new companion to its wonderful predecessor *Children Just Like Me* – introduces us to some of the things children celebrate around the world; it also tells us why and how. It includes religious and other occasions, from cultures and countries as diverse and far apart as India and Zambia, England and Brazil. And again, it sees these joyful events through the eyes and lives and in the words of children themselves – children just like you.

I have taken part in wonderful celebrations of song, dance, and play with children in Asia and Africa in my work for the United Nations Children's Fund. UNICEF seeks to protect children from disease, hunger, exploitation, and abuse, and to ensure that all children have the chance to go to school. A world where every child can develop to his or her fullest potential – wouldn't that be something to celebrate?

I wonder what special days you remember, or are looking forward to. And where did – or will – they take place? Perhaps you would like to write and share *your* favourite celebration with me. I would love to hear from you.

In any event, I hope you enjoy reading this book and sharing the fun of the children who feature in it as much as I have done. May you have something great to celebrate in your life this year!

Katharine

HRH The Duchess of Kent
Patron, UK Committee for UNICEF

About UNICEF

In more than 160 countries, UNICEF helps children – especially the very poorest children – by funding programmes to improve their health, education, and nutrition, and to provide safe drinking water. It also assists children affected by wars and other disasters.

BRITISH AIRWAYS and Change for Good

During UNICEF's 50th birthday celebrations, British Airways employees were honoured with an award for "their outstanding contribution to the cause of UNICEF and the children of the world". The award recognized £4 million donated under the "Change for Good" partnership between UNICEF and British Airways. British Airways is very proud of this continuing partnership and has helped Barnabas and Anabel in their travels for this publication.

Birthdays around the world

MOST OF THE CELEBRATIONS featured in this book are unique to a particular country, or culture, or religion. However, one celebration that most children have in common is their birthday. Around the world, children mark their special day in different ways. In Spain, for example, Alejandra had a party at a bowling alley, to which she invited her friends and classmates, and in Turkey, Ilkay likes to eat cakes called *profiteroles*. Some children, like Suman from India and M'sangombe from Zambia, do not celebrate their birthday because they do not know when it is.

BIRTHDAY PARTY
In many parts of the world, children have a special party to celebrate their birthday. They play games and eat cakes and snacks.

Man Po is nine years old. She was born on 18 November 1987.

Janaina is 12 years old. She was born on 29 October 1984.

M'sangombe thinks he is 10 years old, but is unsure of his exact birth date.

Michal is nine years old. She was born on 4 April 1988.

Sayo is seven years old. She was born on 12 December 1989.

Pratab and Padmini are nine-year-old twins. They were born on 19 July 1988.

Matthew is seven years old. He was born on 2 March 1990.

Matilde is seven years old. She was born on 22 January 1990.

Abi is 10 years old. He was born on 21 June 1987.

Sophie is eight years old. She was born on 21 February 1989.

Ilkay is 10 years old. He was born on 29 January 1987.

Kazu is four years old. He was born on 6 April 1993.

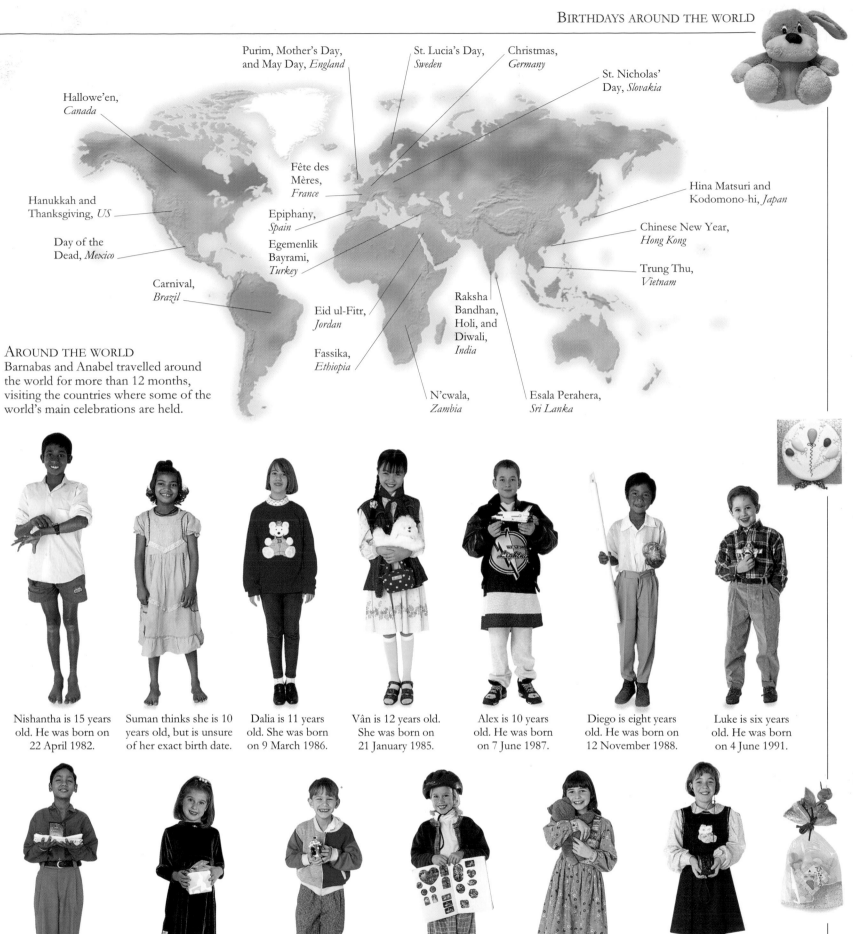

Purim, Mother's Day, and May Day, *England*

St. Lucia's Day, *Sweden*

Christmas, *Germany*

St. Nicholas' Day, *Slovakia*

Hallowe'en, *Canada*

Fête des Mères, *France*

Hina Matsuri and Kodomono-hi, *Japan*

Hanukkah and Thanksgiving, *US*

Epiphany, *Spain*

Chinese New Year, *Hong Kong*

Day of the Dead, *Mexico*

Egemenlik Bayrami, *Turkey*

Trung Thu, *Vietnam*

Carnival, *Brazil*

Raksha Bandhan, Holi, and Diwali, *India*

Eid ul-Fitr, *Jordan*

AROUND THE WORLD
Barnabas and Anabel travelled around the world for more than 12 months, visiting the countries where some of the world's main celebrations are held.

Fassika, *Ethiopia*

N'cwala, *Zambia*

Esala Perahera, *Sri Lanka*

Nishantha is 15 years old. He was born on 22 April 1982.

Suman thinks she is 10 years old, but is unsure of her exact birth date.

Dalia is 11 years old. She was born on 9 March 1986.

Vân is 12 years old. She was born on 21 January 1985.

Alex is 10 years old. He was born on 7 June 1987.

Diego is eight years old. He was born on 12 November 1988.

Luke is six years old. He was born on 4 June 1991.

Sonu is 11 years old. He was born on 10 November 1985.

Isabel is seven years old. She was born on 26 August 1990.

Matús is seven years old. He was born on 23 May 1990.

Karin is nine years old. She was born on 4 June 1988.

Maria is nine years old. She was born on 8 January 1988.

Alejandra is 11 years old. She was born on 22 May 1986.

5

Spring

Springtime festivals share common themes of new life, energy, and growth. For many children, these are happy, colourful festivals that involve flowers, music, and dancing.

Purim
gregger

Fête des Mères card

CHINESE NEW YEAR
• Date: January / February
• Chinese New Year takes place every year between 21 January and 20 February. The exact date is fixed using the Chinese lunar calendar, in which a new moon marks the beginning of each new month.

CARNIVAL
• Date: February
• Religion: Christian
• Carnivals offer people the chance to get together and enjoy themselves before the period of Lent begins. During Lent, Christians remember the 40 days that Jesus spent in the wilderness.

N'CWALA
• Date: February
• Place: Zambia
• In 1835, the Ngoni tribe, an offshoot of the Zulu in South Africa, crossed the Zambezi river into what is now Zambia. This festival celebrates the tribe's good fortune since then, and signals that the harvest can begin.

PURIM
• Date: March
• Religion: Jewish
• The Purim story is about Queen Esther, who saved the Jewish people from massacre by the evil Haman. The name Purim means "lots", and refers to the lots that were drawn to decide the day on which the Jews would be killed.

HINA MATSURI
• Date: third day of third month
• Place: Japan
• This festival comes from the 12th century, when people made paper figures and cast them into water to rid themselves of illness or bad luck. Today's dolls are thought to come from these early paper dolls.

HOLI
• Date: March
• Religion: Hindu
• Holi is celebrated on the day of the full moon in the month of Phalguna (March), when the wheat harvest has been gathered in. Many Hindu legends surround this festival.

MOTHER'S DAY
• Date: March • Religion: Christian
• Also called Mothering Sunday, this festival falls on the fourth Sunday in Lent. It dates back to the Middle Ages, when people in remote villages returned to the main church, or mother church, in their parish for a special service.

FASSIKA (EASTER)
• Date: March / April
• Religion: Christian
• Easter celebrates Jesus' resurrection and is the most important festival for Christians. It falls between 21 March and 25 April, depending on the date of the full moon at the Jewish Passover.

MAY DAY
• Date: first Monday in May
• Place: northern Europe
• For northern Europeans, May Day traditionally marked the first day of spring after the long, harsh months of winter. The day is filled with dancing and flowers to symbolize new growth and life.

These are the children who you will be meeting in this section of the book. They all take part in festivals that occur during the spring months in their country.

Man Po from Hong Kong

Janaina from Brazil

M'sangombe from Zambia

Michal from England

Sayo from Japan

Pratab from India

Matthew from England

Matilde from France

Abi from Ethiopia

Sophie from England

Chinese New Year

MAN PO IS NINE YEARS OLD and lives in Hong Kong. She is looking forward to Chinese New Year, one of the world's most colourful celebrations. Chinese New Year starts on the first day of the Chinese calendar, usually in February. It lasts for 15 days and marks the start of the new year. For many families, it is a time for feasting and visiting relatives and friends, but in the heart of the city, a spectacular procession takes place. The celebrations are based on bringing luck, health, happiness, and wealth throughout the coming year. Chinese families clean their houses thoroughly to rid them of last year's bad luck before the celebrations begin.

STREET PARADE
Thousands of people line the streets of Hong Kong to watch the huge procession of floats in the New Year parade. Dancing dragons and lions weave their way through the crowded streets. The dragon is associated with long life and prosperity. Inside the costume, there can be up to 50 trained martial arts dancers, twisting and turning the dragon's long silk body and blinking its huge eyes.

TERRIFYING OX
According to the Chinese calendar, 1997 is the year of the ox. This imposing ox-shaped float has smoke billowing from its nostrils. This year, there are pictures of the ox all over the city, together with the other New Year decorations.

FIRECRACKERS AT HOME
Chinese people believe that evil spirits dislike loud noises, so Man Po and her family decorate their house with plastic firecrackers. These symbolize the deafening noise that real firecrackers make when they are set off. The noise is intended to frighten away the evil spirits and the bad luck which they might bring.

KUMQUAT TREES
Man Po goes with her parents to the flower market in Hong Kong. At the end of the old year, the market is bustling with people wanting to buy plants and flowers which will bring them good luck in the coming year. The Kumquat tree is considered to be particularly lucky because its Chinese name is a play on the word lucky.

A kumquat looks like a miniature orange, but it tastes a little bit sour.

Kumquat tree

PEACH BLOSSOM
The Chinese believe that peach blossom is lucky. On market stalls, the delicate blossom is wrapped in tissue paper to stop it getting damaged.

COLOURFUL FRUITS
Tangerines with leaves are the lucky fruits of the New Year because of their bright colour. Odd numbers are unlucky, so people always give tangerines in pairs.

Tangerines

Man Po and her family buy their firecracker decorations from a street market stall. They place them in the window or by the doorway in their home so that other people can see them.

People in Hong Kong are not allowed to set off real firecrackers. Instead, they use plastic firecrackers as decorations.

"My outfit is very traditional. It is made of silk and it is very, very beautiful."

"I have written Kung Hei Fat Choy in Chinese, which means 'We hope you get rich'. We say that to everybody at New Year. My family and I visit our grandparents on New Year, and we take sticky rice cakes, called *lin guo*, with us. I look forward most to the red packets that we are given on New Year, because they have money inside them. Each packet contains a different amount of money."

On New Year's Eve, Man Po crushes fragrant lime leaves into her bath water to make sure she is especially clean for the coming year.

Shiny, green lime leaves

Good luck message

Man Po's family name

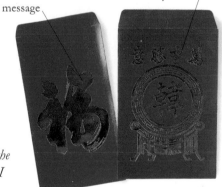

"I save all the money that I am given."

Lucky money packets

LUCKY MONEY
Man Po can hardly wait for New Year's morning when she is given lucky money by her parents and relatives. All Chinese children, and people who are not married, receive money in special red envelopes. Their family name or a good luck message is written on the envelope in gold.

Law pak ko   *Lin guo*

FEAST TREATS
The biggest treats of the New Year celebrations are the sumptuous feasts. For the first day of New Year, Man Po's family try not to eat meat, because each year is named after an animal. On the other days, they can eat whatever they want. Man Po's favourite foods are *law pak ko*, a savoury white carrot cake that contains dried shrimps, and *lin guo*, a sticky rice cake.

Red is the main colour for clothes and decorations at New Year because it is associated with joy and happiness.

CHINESE HOROSCOPE
The ancient Chinese horoscope has been used for thousands of years to analyse a person's character and predict their future. The horoscope works on a 12-year cycle, with each year represented by a different animal. Man Po was born in 1987, which was the year of the rabbit. This means that she is a pleasant, hardworking, and obedient child. When she grows up, she hopes to be tranquil, generous, and imaginative.

RAT
Friendly, intelligent, and polite

OX
Honest, placid, and considerate

TIGER
Competitive, optimistic, a leader

RABBIT
Tranquil, generous, and imaginative

DRAGON
Strong, energetic, and impressive

SNAKE
Elegant, refined, and confident

HORSE
Friendly, eloquent, and loyal

RAM
Gentle, amiable, and sensitive

MONKEY
Independent, astute, and sociable

ROOSTER
Frank, courageous, and good company

DOG
Alert, trustworthy, and faithful

PIG
Calm, tolerant, and optimistic

Carnival

THREE DAYS BEFORE Ash Wednesday in Lent, one of the world's most spectacular Carnivals takes place in Rio de Janeiro, Brazil. Twelve-year-old Janaina is Queen of the Drummers in the Carnival's flamboyant Samba School Parade. Fourteen schools, each with over 3,000 performers, spend the entire year creating elaborate costumes and majestic floats for this magnificent festival. Thousands of people come to watch the colourful procession of performers dancing down one of Rio's grand avenues, to the rhythmic Brazilian music, Samba.

STREET SENSATIONS
While many Brazilians enjoy the grand balls or street parties which take place during Carnival, the highlight of the festivities is undoubtedly the Samba school parade. Thousands of performers, clad in splendid costumes of feathers and beads, dance to the beat of the Samba drums along the grand parade avenue. The dancing continues inside the Sambadrome, a specially designed dance stadium that holds up to 85,000 people.

MANGUEIRA SAMBA SCHOOL
The Mangueira Samba school is the oldest Samba school. Janaina belongs to the Mangueira do Amanhã, which is for children and teenagers. Every Samba school has its own colours and its own supporters. Mangueira's colours are pink and green and its logo is of a mango tree, because *mangueira* is Portuguese for mango.

Mangueira do Amanhã logo. The school's name means mango of the future.

FLAG CARRIER
Every Samba school has a female flag bearer, called the *Porta Bandeira*. She is always accompanied by a male dancer. One of the flag bearers at Janaina's school is just three years old.

MAKING THE COSTUMES
Months of preparation go into designing the costumes for the parade, but the theme remains a secret until the very last moment. Hundreds of people living near Samba schools help to make the costumes, sticking sequins and sewing ornaments on to each and every garment.

"I learned to dance Samba by watching people."

"All of my moves are designed to tell the story."

"The dance rehearsals for this Carnival began in December."

SAMBA STORIES
A prize is awarded every year to the best Samba school and competition between the schools is fierce. Each Samba school develops its own story and choreography for the parade. Costumes are specially designed and samba songs are composed to match the Samba school's chosen theme. Distinct groups, called *alas* (wings), tell the different parts of the school's story.

Sebastião is a drummer in the parade.

These bright orange headdresses are for the female dancers, called *Bainnas*, who honour the history of the parade.

FLOAT MAKING
For almost four months, people from the community work on the floats, building sculptures out of fibreglass and styrofoam. Everybody works hard because they want their Samba school to win the competition.

Each school can have up to 80 drummers.

CARNAVAL

"I like wearing this feathered headdress as it looks like those that the big Mangueira dancers wear."

"I don't usually see my Carnival costume until the day before, when I try it on to see if it fits."

"My costume has silver tassles which shake when I dance. It was made especially for me."

"There are so many Samba songs that I don't have a favourite."

"My name is Janaina. I belong to the Mangueira do Amanhã Samba school. I live close by, in a *favela* (shanty town). I have been a Samba dancer in the Carnival since I was five years old. My favourite part of the Carnival is when I am dancing down the avenue. I feel more than happy, I feel amazed that the Carnival is so big. When it is all over, I just have to think that next year there's another one."

Coconut milk is a favourite drink.

Pineapple

CARNIVAL FOOD

The name Carnival comes from the words "Carne Vale", which mean goodbye to meat. During the 40 days of Lent, Christians are not supposed to eat meat or other rich foods. Traditionally, Carnival was seen as the last chance to feast before this period. Janaina's favourite Carnival foods are those from the street stalls around the city, such as pineapples, fried chicken parcels, and *linguiça*.

Guava

Chicken parcels

Pipoca (pink popcorn)

Linguiça (sausage on a stick)

"We have rehearsals for our part in the parade every Monday."

"My feet ache after hours of dancing Samba."

Camille is a flag bearer in the parade.

CARNIVAL AWARD

Seven Samba schools appear on each night of the parade. The flamboyant spectacle begins at 7 pm on the Sunday, and continues late into the night. The winning Samba school receives a prestigious award and money from the government to help them prepare for next year's carnival.

N'cwala

M'SANGOMBE IS A 10-YEAR-OLD Ngoni warrior from the Eastern Province in Zambia. This year he was chosen to dance at the N'cwala ceremony, which is held each February to celebrate the harvest. The festival is based on the Ngoni tradition of offering the Paramount Ngoni chief the first produce of the year. Twelve local chiefs from the Eastern Province travel with their finest dancers to the village of Mutenguleni, where the ceremony takes place. Each group dances before the Paramount chief, and he elects one group as the best warrior dancers.

THE PARAMOUNT CHIEF
The Paramount Ngoni chief in Eastern Zambia is Chief M'pzeni. He is seen as king among the Ngoni and rules the 12 chiefs of the surrounding villages. Each year, he travels to the N'cwala with his royal entourage. He watches and takes part in the dancing. He drinks the blood of a cow killed at the N'cwala as a symbol of the first harvest food, and as a blessing for his people to start harvesting and eating.

DANCING DISPLAYS
The N'cwala ceremony takes place in a field. Each of the 12 groups of dancers perform their powerful warrior dance to show how they would protect the Paramount chief if they were at war.

WARRIOR DANCE
In the past, if a Ngoni warrior was a good, strong, and aggressive dancer, he would be thought of as an able warrior. M'sangombe was therefore very excited to be chosen to dance before the Paramount chief, because it meant that he may one day become a fearsome warrior.

"My favourite part of my costume is my N'kholi, because I dance with it."

PRACTISING THE DANCING
People start arriving at Mutenguleni the day before the ceremony and some of the groups start practising their dancing. During the practice, M'sangombe has the privilege of dancing with the head of his village, Chief M'nukwa.

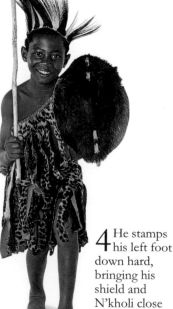

"I repeat these movements over and over again during the dance."

"My shield is to protect me from things like spears."

"I dance with my grandfather at the N'cwala."

1 First, M'sangombe lifts his right knee up, holds his N'kholi (stick) up high, and his shield away from him.

2 He stamps his right foot heavily on the ground, bends his knees, and brings his N'kholi and shield down to protect him.

3 M'sangombe pulls his left knee high into the air and thrusts his N'kholi upwards.

4 He stamps his left foot down hard, bringing his shield and N'kholi close to his body.

N'CWALA

M'sangombe's headdress is made from the bristly hair of a zebra's mane. It is attached to a band made from animal skin.

"This is the first time that I have danced in the N'cwala. I am the youngest person in my group. All my friends have stayed in the village. On the bus journey to the N'cwala I was very excited. The Chief of my village was also on the bus. I am not afraid of him, but I respect him because he is a Chief. If I had the chance to be a Chief, I would be excited and happy. I would look after the people in my Chiefdom."

The shield is called a Chishango. It is made from cow hide and fur and has a stick at the back for holding it. Traditionally a child's costume would have been made entirely from cow hide.

The leopard skin garment around M'sangombe's shoulder is tassled in the traditional warrior style.

The women clap their hands as they sing, to create a rhythm for the warrior's dance.

FOOD FOR A CHIEF
The Paramount chief stays at a nearby village for the N'cwala. The villagers give up their homes for the chief and his royal party to stay in. During the ceremony, some of the women from the visiting villages prepare a large pot of beef stew for the chief.

The garment around M'sangombe's waist is artificial fur. Most of the warriors wear real animal furs.

"My grandfather made my outfit. When he was younger, he went into the bush to hunt for the animals."

WOMEN SUPPORTERS
Ngoni women form a circle around their men as they dance, clapping and singing songs of encouragement, to boost the men's morale for impending battles. At the N'cwala, women sing songs about how strong and fierce their group of dancers is.

Corn

Every Ngoni has to carry a stick called a N'kholi. It is made from a hard wood, and is the sign of a warrior.

"I don't need to wear shoes, as I am used to having bare feet."

WOMEN SELLING CORN
One of the most readily available foods in Zambia is corn. Most people grow their own corn, which they eat steamed or make into a dish called maize meal. These women are selling corn to people at the N'cwala.

Purim

NINE-YEAR-OLD MICHAL and her friends are Jewish and come from London in England. During the Jewish month of *Adar*, between February and March, they celebrate Purim. This happy festival tells the story of Queen Esther, who saved the Jews from being massacred by an evil man named Haman. Children wear fancy dress and perform plays of the Purim story. Families attend a service at the synagogue, and afterwards enjoy delicious Purim pastries and breads.

SWAPPING PURIM GIFTS
At Purim, it is a Jewish custom to exchange gifts with friends. Children often make special giftboxes, which they fill with fruit or sweets. This custom of sending gifts is called *Mishloach Manot*.

This year, Adam (the King in the play) gave a box to Michal (Esther).

"My name is Michal. I am dressed up as a hippy, but I was chosen to be Esther in the play."

"My name is Rupert. I am nine years old. I have dressed up as James Bond, but in the play I am Mordechai."

THE PURIM STORY
Purim is about a Persian King called Ahasueros, who was married to a woman called Vashti.

1 One day, he summoned Vashti, but she refused to appear. Furious, the King left Vashti and married a woman named Esther. Unbeknown to the King, Esther was a Jew.

2 The King's chief adviser was a man named Haman. Haman hated the Jews, in particular Esther's uncle, Mordechai, who refused to bow down to him. When Haman ordered that all the Jews be killed, Mordechai pleaded with Esther to tell the King.

3 Esther asked the King and Haman to dine with her. At dinner, she revealed that she was Jewish, and that Haman wanted to kill her and her people. The King was shocked and angry. Though Haman begged Esther to spare his life, he was sent to the gallows.

Haman throws himself at Esther's feet to beg for mercy.

"My name is Max. I am dressed up as a flight lieutenant, but in the play I am Haman. Haman is the best character because he gets lots of attention."

Purim

Rattle, or *gregger*

"Purim is a lively spring festival. I liked doing the play this year because it was really funny. We had all these songs to learn, which took me about three days. I was chosen to be Esther, because as a girl, you could only be Esther or Vashti. We always wear fancy dress at Purim and for the play, we wear sashes to show which characters we are. My favourite character in the play is definitely Haman, because he's really evil but everybody boos at him, so he's also a fun character."

Clown *gregger*

WATCHING THE PLAY

The Purim story comes from the Book of Esther in the Bible, and is often written as a scroll called the Megillat Esther. When it is read out at the synagogue, the listeners boo and hiss each time Haman's name is mentioned. When the play is performed in schools, children stamp their feet and shake their homemade *greggers* (rattles) when Haman appears. By making such a tremendous noise, the children are trying to wipe out Haman's name.

"My name is Adam. I am eight years old. I play King Ahasueros, but I'm dressed as a secret agent, because the clothes are really cool."

This Purim rattle is made of cardboard and filled with beads or buttons.

"I am Vashti in the play, but my real name is Odette. I am eight years old. My fancy dress costume is Florence Nightingale."

PURIM FOODS

People eat two types of food at Purim. *Hamantashen* are small triangular-shaped pastries, which are meant to represent Haman's ears or his pockets. *Purim Challah* is a large braided loaf, which is sprinkled with tiny specks of different colored sugar icing or poppy seeds. Michal's family buys these cakes from their local bakery.

Hamantashen

Purim Challah

Hina Matsuri

EVERY YEAR, SEVEN-YEAR-OLD SAYO from Osaka in Japan looks forward to 3 March when Hina Matsuri takes place – a day dedicated entirely to dolls. Nearly every Japanese girl owns a special set of beautiful dolls, which has either been bought especially for her, or has been in her family for many years. The dolls are considered too precious to play with. Instead, they are displayed in the best room in the house, which is usually the Tatami room. The dolls represent traditional Japanese values, such as calmness and dignity, and are intended to set an example that young girls can follow.

AWASHIMA SHRINE
The Japanese believe that a person's illness or bad luck can be transferred to a doll. They therefore hold a purification ceremony each year during Hina Matsuri at the Awashima Shrine near Osaka. Families who are worried about their children's health or well-being donate dolls to the shrine. Shinto priests offer special prayers before casting the dolls out to sea in wooden boats.

CEREMONY OF DOLLS
Huge crowds gather outside the shrine to watch the ceremony, which is called *Nagashi-Bina* (casting the dolls out to sea). The dolls are placed in the boats, and after prayers have been said, the boats are led in a procession from the shrine to the nearby sea. Shintoists dressed in religious Japanese robes chant prayers as they follow the path down to the sea.

In shops and stalls throughout Japan, small models of Hina dolls are sold during the festival. Some of the dolls contain sweets or savoury snacks.

People carry flowers which they place in the boats.

The boats are piled high with different dolls.

CARRYING THE BOAT
Each boat is tightly packed with hundreds of traditional Japanese dolls. The boats are so heavy that at least eight people are needed to carry each one.

LOWERING THE BOATS
On the jetty, the carriers gently lower the boats to the ground. Before the dolls are pushed out to sea, Japanese Shintoists carry out traditional rituals and purification prayers on them. The boats are tied together with rope to stop them drifting apart at sea.

Ropes help the boats to stay together at sea.

SAILING AWAY
After the prayers are completed, the boats are set afloat in the water. As the three vessels drift out to sea with the miniature dolls inside, their owners believe that any ill-fortune they may have suffered is carried away with them. For this reason, these dolls are often called "casting-off dolls".

Some people believe that the dolls go to the country of gods.

ひなまつり

"My grandparents gave me this kimono. It has so many layers, which makes it quite uncomfortable to wear."

"I have written Hina Matsuri, in Japanese. Hina means 'small doll'. My grandparents gave me my set of dolls when I was born. The dolls are not for playing with, they are only to look at. I am still too young to arrange my doll display, because the dolls are very precious, so my mother does it. It takes her about an hour and she makes the display look like an Emperor's palace. I help her to clean the room and when I am 14 years old, I will set up the dolls myself."

Sayo's favourite doll is the beautiful Empress. The Empress is dressed in ceremonial court robes, which are made up of 12 layers of silk.

A red cotton cloth covers the steps of the elaborate display.

SAYO'S DOLL DISPLAY
Ten days before the festival, Sayo and her mother clean the best room of the house and erect a seven-tiered platform. On the highest step, Sayo's mother places the Emperor and Empress dolls. Beneath them are the rest of the palace staff and on the bottom steps is the palace furniture.

DOLL'S FURNITURE
An elaborate lacquered chest of drawers and a table containing traditional Japanese tableware furnish the covered steps. To represent the season of this festival, each display must also contain a cherry blossom tree and a mandarin tree.

Cherry blossom tree

Table with bowls

Chest of drawers

TASTY SNACKS
One of the traditional foods for Hina Matsuri is pink rice cakes, called *mochi*, which are wrapped in cherry (*sakura*) blossom leaves. These seasonal treats are called *sakura mochi*. Cakes and snacks are also prepared and offered first to the dolls and then to visitors.

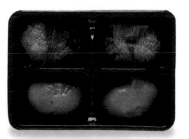

Bag of snacks with Hina dolls on top

"These cakes have whipped cream and strawberries inside them. They are so tasty!"

"I must put my dolls away on the first weekend after Hina Matsuri, or else I might not get married at the right age."

"I love sitting and looking at my dolls."

Sakura mochi

Pratab

Holi

PRATAB AND PADMINI ARE nine-year-old twins, who live in Rajasthan in northwest India. Each year, the twins celebrate Holi, their favourite springtime festival. Holi is a Hindu festival that takes place in early March, when the wheat harvest is gathered in. Two different stories are remembered at Holi. One is about the god Krishna and the other is about Prahlad and the wicked Holika, after whom the festival is named. The night before Holi, people light fires to rid the air of evil spirits. The next morning, chaos reigns as people cover themselves and each other in brightly coloured powders.

KRISHNA AND RADHA
People remember the god Krishna and his beloved companion Radha at Holi. Legend has it that Krishna loved to play tricks on Radha and her friends, the *gopis* (milkmaids). At Holi, he used to drench them with coloured water and steal their clothes as they bathed.

Green powder

Pink powder

Orange powder

Yellow powder

Red powder

STALLS OF COLOUR
Wooden carts heaped with mounds of brightly coloured powdered paints line the streets of northern India during Holi. These powdered paints are called *gulal*. In the past they were made from vegetable and other natural dyes, like turmeric, and the colours were limited to shades of red, orange, and yellow. Today, the powders are mixed with chemicals to produce colours such as mauve, blue, silver, and gold. Pratab and Padmini begin the festivities by smearing dry colours on one another, before moving on to coloured water paints.

WATER SQUIRTERS
Krishna is said to have used a brass syringe, called a *pichkari*, to squirt coloured water over Radha. Children today use a variety of objects, from plastic bottles to water pistols. Pratab, Padmini, and their family use silver bicycle pumps to spray their water colours.

Stall selling water squirters

"I love Holi because it's the only time we're allowed to be dirty. I like getting clean afterwards though."

Pratab and Padmini's bicycle pump

"I like to mix all the powders together and make a big mess!"

LADDU STALL
The Holi festivities end in the afternoon and Pratab and Padmini go inside to scrub off the coloured paint. They spend the rest of the day relaxing with their family and eating Indian sweets such as *laddu*.

Stall selling *laddu*

Laddu is made from split pea flour and sugar syrup.

Padmini

"I don't like the dirty silver colour. My uncle put it all over my face and I had to wash it hard to get it off."

"My sister Padmini has written Holi in Hindi. On the night before Holi, we dressed up in our best clean clothes and we watched the Holi bonfire. We moved away from the fire when our uncle pulled out the stick, because the flames were so big. The next morning, we put on our old clothes, so our best clothes don't get colour all over them. Then we cover each other in brightly coloured powders. We play for hours with our friends, soaking each other in red water colour."

The tree branch represents Prahlad.

THE LEGEND OF PRAHLAD

Prahlad was the son of King Hiranyakashyap, who wanted his subjects to worship him instead of God. Prahlad refused and the King ordered him to be killed. However, God always saved Prahlad. The King's wicked sister Holika built a huge bonfire and led Prahlad into the flames. She thought she had magical powers to protect her, but she died and Prahlad was saved.

HOLI BONFIRE

Families build large bonfires on the night before Holi to remind them of Prahlad and of how good always triumphs over evil. They place a large tree branch in the middle of the fire to represent Prahlad. Once the fire is burning, they remove the stick, as if to save him.

Small stalls sell garlands of cow dung, which are placed inside the Holi bonfire. In India, the cow is a sacred animal and its dung is holy.

"It takes two days for the colour to come off completely. The worst colours are bright pink and blue."

"After lunch it's nice to be clean again."

WATER COLOUR FIGHT

Having covered each other with coloured powder, Pratab and Padmini fill up their bicycle pumps with red coloured water. Then the real fun begins!

"I don't like to mix the colours together, I like to keep them all separate."

A few hours later, it's difficult to recognize anybody! The twins, their friends, and their relatives are all drenched with red water. After the fun is over, everyone goes inside to get clean.

Mother's Day

SEVEN-YEAR-OLD MATTHEW lives in London, England. Each year on Mother's Day, he makes a special card and buys a beautiful bunch of spring flowers to give to his mother. This Christian festival is also called Mothering Sunday and it falls on the fourth Sunday in Lent. In the past, it was a time to relax the rigid rules of Lent and for working people to go home and see their mothers.

Narcissi

MOTHER'S DAY FLOWERS
Pale yellow narcissi are plentiful in England during spring. Matthew chose them for Mother's Day because of their sweet smell.

Matthew gave his mother Katherine a delicious box of chocolates.

"I like these narcissus flowers because they look like tiny daffodils."

"I would like to make my mummy a cup of tea, but I'm too young to pour the hot water."

"After going to church, we'll take mummy for a picnic in our local park."

"We celebrate Mother's Day because mummy works so hard. She cooks me supper and lunch. Mummy does everything in fact, she does all the washing up and even the ironing. Most of all, she gives me love and looks after me when I'm ill."

Matthew made a card for his mother at school. He used yellow tissue paper for the row of daffodils and cut the shiny green leaves out of a sheet of cellophane.

HAPPY MOTHERS DAY

GOING TO CHURCH
Most churches in England have a special service on Mother's Day. This dates back to the Middle Ages, when people returned to their main, or mother, church for a special service. Matthew goes to the church close to his school with his mother, brother Daniel, and father Richard. There they sing hymns and say prayers for all mothers.

"On Mother's Day, I try to be good and tidy, and put away all my toys."

Fête des Mères

BEFORE THE LAST SUNDAY in May each year, seven-year-old Matilde from Toulouse in France spends days drawing a card and practising a poem as a surprise for her mother. This springtime Sunday is called Fête des Mères, and it provides children and adults throughout France with the opportunity to make their mother the centre of attention, and give her gifts and treats.

"I call my mother maman, which is mummy in French."

"Papa and I hide our presents for maman until the Sunday."

BREAKFAST TRAY
For Fête des Mères, Matilde prepares her mother's favourite breakfast and serves it on a tray. She makes *tartine* (slice of bread) with blackcurrant jam and a cup of tea.

Roses — Tartine with blackcurrant jam — Tea

BREAKFAST IN BED
Usually Matilde's mother is awake long before her children, preparing their breakfast. As a special treat on Fête des Mères, Matilde gets up before her mother and brings her breakfast in bed. She also recites the poem she has learned and gives her flowers and a card.

fête des mamans

"I call this day Mummy's Festival, which I have written here in French. Every day maman wakes me up with a big kiss, but on this day, I take her breakfast in bed, give her flowers and a card, then I recite a poem about how much I love her. My favourite part of the day is when we eat the *gâteau*."

GORGEOUS *GATEAU*
Matilde went to her favourite *pâtisserie* to buy this beautiful cake for her mother. They will eat it in the afternoon, because it is too rich to eat in the morning.

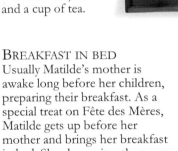

Roses are a symbol of love, and this is the bouquet that Matilde gave her mother this year.

Matilde drew a picture of her mother on the card that she made for her at school.

Matilde has written out her favourite poem and decorated it with pictures of flowers.

"I love maman because when I am sad she comforts me."

"Maman loves the drawings that I've done for her."

ST. GEORGE'S CHURCH
This is the Ethiopian Orthodox Christian (*Tewahido*) church that Abi goes to. The round dome on the roof is typical of Orthodox churches. On the eve of Easter Sunday, everybody attends the special service of chanting and drumming which continues into the early hours of Easter morning.

Fassika

ABI IS TEN YEARS OLD and lives in Addis Ababa in Ethiopia. He is an Orthodox Christian and to him, the most important festival of the whole year is Fassika, or Easter. This festival celebrates the day when Jesus Christ rose from the dead after being crucified. Christians worldwide celebrate Easter, but Orthodox Christians follow the ancient Orthodox calendar, which means that they celebrate Easter on a later date than Christians in the west.

Palm crown with a cross in the middle

Abi's rings of woven palm leaves

CANDLE SELLER
Women sit outside each of the churchyards selling candles to the congregation. The candles are called *twaf* and are made from thin threads of cotton bound together with a small amount of wax.

ABI HOLDING CANDLES
For Christians, the flame of a candle represents the light of Jesus Christ. During the Easter service, everybody buys a candle and lights it from one that is already burning. At the end of the service, the congregation, with its candles lit, follows the priests who make a tour around the outside of the church.

Candles, or *twaf*

PALM SUNDAY (*HOSAINA*)
The Sunday before Easter is called Palm Sunday. This day marks the beginning of Holy Week (the last week of Jesus' life) and celebrates the story of Jesus riding into Jerusalem on a donkey. Ethiopians wear headbands of palm leaves on this day to remind them of the palm leaves that were laid in Jesus' path. Abi makes his own special crown with a cross in the middle. He also weaves elaborate rings out of palm leaves.

IN CHURCH
The Easter service begins at about 8 o'clock on Saturday evening and lasts until about 3 o'clock on Sunday morning. The congregation, including Abi and his family, attends the entire service. Ethiopians wear traditional white clothes, called *yabesha libs*, for the Easter service.

CHURCH SERVICE
All night long, the priests chant prayers in an ancient Ethiopian language called Ge'ez. At about 10 o'clock at night, the drummers begin to beat their drums to accompany the chanting. The congregation prays as it listens to the soothing sound of the chanting.

"I like wearing my crown because I have made the front in the shape of the cross. The cross reminds me of Jesus."

"I like Fassika because it's a holiday."

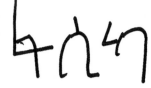

"I have written Fassika, which is the name for Ethiopian Easter. On this day we celebrate our Lord Jesus having risen from the dead. For almost two months before Fassika, my whole family doesn't eat meat or anything that comes from an animal. I am a bit too young to fast properly, but I don't eat meat because there is none at home. When I go to church on Easter eve, I pray to the Lord. I ask him to protect me from those who might harm me and I thank him for everything."

PICTURES OF JESUS
Abi's family have hung many pictures of Jesus Christ on the walls of their house. Jesus is very important to them. They believe that Jesus is the Son of God and that he guides and protects them.

"One of my favourite parts of the church service is the chanting."

For their celebratory meal on Easter Sunday, Abi and his family eat *injera* with a mutton stew called *beg wot*. *Injera* is a large sourdough pancake, made from a special type of flour, called *tef*.

A type of cottage cheese called *aib* is sprinkled on the *injera*.

Mutton stew, or *beg wot*

The *injera* is also eaten with *dulet*, or chopped spiced lamb tripe and liver.

FASSIKA FAMILY MEAL
The period before Easter Sunday is called Lent. During Lent, Ethiopian Christians avoid any animal products, such as meat, eggs, butter, milk, yoghurt, cream, and cheese. After they have been to the Easter eve service, Abi and his family return home to break their fast and later in the afternoon, they share the main celebratory meal of the day.

"My shirt is called ejetebab. I like wearing it because of the embroidery in the middle."

Abi's family serves their *dabo* on a tall wicker stool called a *mesob*.

CUTTING *DABO*
During all their holidays, Ethiopians eat a huge special sourdough bread called *dabo*. They bake enough to offer a slice to everybody who visits the house. On Easter morning, the bread should be cut, after saying a prayer, by a priest, if one is present, or by the main man of the house. Today, Abi cut the bread, because the other men of the house were not present.

May Day

SOPHIE IS EIGHT YEARS OLD and lives near the small village of Ickwell in the heart of the English countryside. On 1 May each year, Sophie and other children from nearby villages gather to celebrate May Day, a festival that marks the arrival of spring after the harsh winter months. The day is filled with music and flowers and at the centre of the celebrations is an enormous stripy maypole, around which the children dance.

MAYPOLE
Ickwell is one of the last villages in England where a maypole stands all year round. Ickwell's maypole was built in 1894 and is made from a fir tree. In the past, ship's masts were often used as maypoles.

In her drawing, Sophie has shown the Ickwell maypole covered with colourful ribbons.

On May Day, last year's May Queen is paraded through the village before she passes her crown and throne on to the new Queen.

MAY QUEEN ELECTION
Each May Day, a May Queen is chosen to reign over the festivities. The Queen is crowned on a flower-covered throne and is accompanied by a group of children, called attendants. Sophie and other children from the village vote for the prettiest girl in their area.

COUNTRY DANCING
May Day is filled with lively music and country dancing. This year, for the first time, Sophie took part in the country dancing. She had to learn the different dances at school, which took about three months, and was taught by two women who were also involved in the festival when they were children. The children here are performing the Ribbon Dance.

CUMBERLAND SQUARE
Sophie's favourite May Day dance is called the Cumberland Square. Traditionally, each girl should have a boy as a partner. However, in Sophie's school there are not enough boys, so Sophie's partner is her best friend, Rebecca. The dancers begin by honouring their partners with a curtsy and then skip around in a circle holding hands.

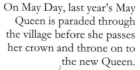

"First we curtsy to honour our partners."

"We cross hands with our partners."

"We skip in one direction, and then the other."

"I put these beautiful green leaves on my hoop first, because green is my favourite colour."

"On May Day we wear plimsolls or trainers. They are easier to dance in because the rubber soles stop you from slipping on the grass."

May Day

"One day when I'm old enough, I would like to be the May Queen, but this year I'm a country dancer. When I woke up, I was so excited about May Day. Then I made my hoop and that made me calm down a bit, because it made me think, I'll pick this flower and then I'll pick that. I love May Day because it reminds me of spring and I can hear the birds sing in my garden. I would like to celebrate May Day until I'm grown up."

"My dress is made of thin material so I don't get hot when I dance."

Grape hyacinth

Cowslip

Pansy

Dandelion

"These pink flowers are Daddy's favourite."

"I stuck the flowers on to my spotty headband."

HEAD GARLAND
Each girl makes her own head garland. Sophie is lucky because she lives in the country, so she has hundreds of flowers to choose from. She stuck her favourite ones on to her headband. This took quite a long time, so Sophie kept all the flowers in a bucket of water to stop them dying.

Primula

"A special lady makes all our dresses and they are kept in a box until May Day, when we each choose a dress that fits us."

NEW BUDS
After the long cold winter, in which the trees look dead and bare, the spring sunshine encourages tiny green buds to appear at the end of each twig and branch. The buds protect tightly furled new leaves until they have grown enough to burst through.

Sophie decorated her story with pictures of maypoles and flowers.

Among the flowers that Sophie used for her hoop were two different kinds of daffodil.

A COLOURFUL HOOP
A competition is held each May Day for the prettiest hoop. All the girls are given a wooden hoop, which they decorate elaborately with spring flowers. Sophie covered her hoop with grey and red ribbons, to which she then attached lots of different flowers.

HAPPY DAY
Here, Sophie has written out the story of her May Day. She describes what she did from the moment she woke up, including picking the flowers with her brother for her hoop and the dancing that took place on the village green.

MAY DAY TRADITIONS
One of the most popular May Day traditions is the weaving of ribbons around the Maypole. This custom appeared in England in the 1890s and is believed to have come from Southern Europe. As the children dance in and out, the ribbons are woven into a colourful plait, like this red, white, and blue one. When the children change direction, the ribbons unwind, symbolizing the lengthening of the days.

MORRIS DANCERS
These boisterous male folk dancers are a familiar sight in many parts of England on May Day. Morris dancers are named after 13th century Spanish "Moresco" dancers, who blackened their faces so that evil powers could not recognize them. Today's Morris dancers do not always blacken their faces, but they do stamp their feet, clash sticks, and wave large handkerchiefs when they dance, to represent the triumph of summer (good) over winter (evil).

FLOWERED HAT
Morris dancers decorate their straw hats with fresh flowers to represent the coming of spring and fresh, new life.

BALDRICKS
Every group of Morris dancers wears braces of different colours, called "baldricks". The colours of the baldricks show which district or town the dancers belong to. These blue and yellow baldricks are from a town called Letchworth in the heart of England.

ANKLE BELLS
Morris dancers wear these bells around their ankles. The loud jangling sound that they make as the men dance is intended to ward off evil.

Summer

Summertime festivals share common themes of long, hot days and plentiful food. Children look forward to spending time with their family and to playing outdoors with their friends.

Carp kite

Offerings for Raksha Bandhan

EGEMENLIK BAYRAMI
• Date: 23 April • Place: Turkey
• This festival was begun in 1920 by the founder of modern Turkey, Mustafa Kemal Atatürk. He recognized how important children were to his country's future and dedicated this day to them.

KODOMONO-HI
• Date: fifth day of fifth month • Place: Japan
• Families fly huge, carp-shaped kites from their houses on this day. The Japanese regard the carp fish as a symbol of success, and it is used as an example of the qualities that young Japanese boys should develop.

ESALA PERAHERA
• Date: Esala (August) • Religion: Buddhist
• This Sri Lankan festival honours the Sacred Tooth, or Holy Relic, of the Lord Buddha in elaborate processions that set out from the shrines of the Hindu gods Natha, Vishnu, and Kataragama, and the goddess Pattini.

RAKSHA BANDHAN
• Date: August • Origin: India
• This festival celebrates the love between brothers and sisters and involves a sister giving her brother a bracelet of woven threads, called a *rakhi*. This tradition dates back 500 years, when sisters tied *rakhis* on their brothers' wrist to protect them on the battlefield. In turn, the brothers vowed to protect their sisters' honour from foreign invaders.

MOVEABLE FESTIVALS:

EID UL-FITR
• Date: moveable • Religion: Muslim
• The Muslim calendar is lunar, which means that each new month begins with a new moon. There are no fixed seasonal Muslim festivals because the calendar moves back through the seasons by about 11 days each year. The ninth month, Ramadan, is a holy month for Muslims, during which they avoid all food and drink between sunrise and sunset. Muslims celebrate the end of this fast with the festival of Eid ul-Fitr, when they give thanks to Allah for his help during the fast.

These are the children who you will be meeting in this section of the book. They all take part in festivals that occur during the summer months in their country.

Ilkay from Turkey   Kazu from Japan   Nishantha from Sri Lanka   Suman from India   Dalia from Jordan

Egemenlik Bayrami

ILKAY IS TEN YEARS OLD and lives in the Turkish city of Istanbul. On 23 April each year, the people of Turkey celebrate Egemenlik Bayrami, or Independence Holiday. This one-day holiday is also dedicated to children and was declared by the famous Turkish leader, Atatürk, in 1920. All over the country, schoolchildren dress up in national costumes or fancy dress and perform plays. The main event takes place in Ankara, Turkey's capital city, where children from around the world are invited to take part in a spectacular display of singing and dancing.

Atatürk's monument in Istanbul

ATATURK
Mustafa Kemal was the founder of the modern state of Turkey after the collapse of the Ottoman Empire in 1913. He was known as Atatürk, which means "father of the Turks". He ruled Turkey for 15 years and introduced many reforms.

This scout is holding a branch to represent the trees that the scouts will plant.

ENVIRONMENTAL SCOUTS
During the Egemenlik Bayrami celebrations, scouts plant young trees. The trees are to remind adults and children of environmental issues.

ATATURK'S MEMORIAL
A memorial service for Atatürk takes place just before the main Egemenlik Bayrami celebrations begin. People lay flowers in front of his monument, sing the national anthem, and observe a minute's silence.

ISTANBUL
In Istanbul, where Ilkay lives, the national football stadium is the venue for a grand children's event. Children put on fantastic displays of songs, poems, and specially choreographed dances in honour of children and of the festival's founder, Atatürk.

TURKISH NATIONAL DRESS
During Egemenlik Bayrami, many Turkish children dress up in their national costume and proudly display a part of their culture. In some parts of eastern Turkey, people still wear the national costume, but most people today favour western clothes.

Sequined hat, or *tepelik*

White shirt, or *gömlek*

Colourful waistcoat, or *yelek*

Baggy trousers, or *şalvar*

This costume has an elaborate sequined veil, or *başlik*.

The long gown is called a *kaftan*.

This is one of the most famous Turkish costumes.

Costume from Artvin, near the Black Sea

Costumes from Sivas in mid-Turkey

Costume from Erzincan in eastern Turkey

Costume from Artvin, near the Black Sea

Dancer from Diyarbakir in south eastern Turkey

Egemenlik Bayrami

"This year, the theme of our school musical was the Olympics. I played a Turkish wrestler. I love sports and I am really proud to be a wrestler. Each year we wear different costumes for Egemenlik Bayrami, and I have also been a naval officer. But the wrestling costume is definitely my favourite. I don't get any presents at Egemenlik, just having a holiday is a present to me. I remember Atatürk at this time. He is my hero, and he made this holiday especially for all the children."

"I watched the children's festival in Ankara on TV. I saw children from China dancing. I like seeing children from other countries. It makes me want to visit those places."

"At Egemenlik Bayrami, we sing songs. My favourite song is about Atatürk. He was the most important Turk of all."

"My mother's cousin is a wrestler. I would like to be a wrestler, too."

"Before Egemenlik Bayrami, we had lots of rehearsals for the national dances and the waltzes that we have to perform."

The emblem on Ilkay's wrestling outfit is the Turkish flag.

"This is a picture of me when I was five years old. I loved the colourful sash of my costume."

ILKAY'S NATIONAL DRESS
Ilkay has taken part in the Egemenlik Bayrami celebrations since he was five years old. For his first school performance, he dressed up in a national costume from the Black Sea area of Turkey.

Burma

STREET STALLS
Outside the stadiums in each of Turkey's main cities, street vendors sell meatballs called *köfte*. The *köfte* are grilled and served with tomato, in *pide* bread. *Pide* is unleavened bread, which means it is made without yeast and therefore does not rise. This delicious Turkish sandwich is ideal for eating while watching the festivities.

Şekarpare

Simit seller

TURKISH SNACKS AND SWEETS
Another tasty snack found outside the stadiums and in the city streets is *simit*. This is a round salty ring of dough, covered in sesame seeds. Many people also eat sticky Turkish sweets made with pistachio nuts and honey, such as *şekarpare* and *burma*.

The dough is twisted into a ring shape and sprinkled with sesame seeds before it is baked.

Simit

Kodomono-hi

FOUR-YEAR-OLD KAZU lives in Osaka in Japan. Each year, on the fifth day of May, Kazu and other Japanese boys look forward to Kodomono-hi, or Children's Day. On this day, families with young boys fly colourful streamers and enormous kites, in the shape of carp fish, from a large pole in the garden. Inside the houses families display traditional warrior dolls and bathe the children in iris leaves. The main purpose of this festival is to demonstrate to young boys the importance of qualities such as strength and determination.

FLYING KITES
On 5 May, brightly coloured streamers and carp kites fly above rooftops all over Japan. The kites are attached to a long bamboo pole, which has a windmill at the top. Beneath the windmill, long strands of colourful streamers, called *fuki-nagashi*, float in the wind. The streamers and carp kites symbolize a family; the first kite represents a father, the second represents a mother, and the third represents a child.

The windmill is called the *kaza-gurama*, and it moves around in the breeze.

こいのぼり

CARP SIGNATURE
Kazu has written *Koinobori*, which is a name for the colourful streamers and carp kites. *Koi* means carp.

These strands of colourful streamers are called *fuki-nagashi*. They represent freedom in life.

"When my mother and father were children, the streamers were made out of silk, but mine are made out of nylon."

"We put our carp streamers on a pole on our verandah."

As the wind flows through the carp's large open mouth, the kite fills out and appears to swim in the air, like a real fish.

CARP KITES
The carp is a strong, robust fish, renowned for its energy and determination as it swims upstream against the current and jumps high out of the water. The carp therefore provides a good example to Japanese boys, who must also overcome obstacles and be successful. Carp kites come in different sizes and prices, depending on how they are made. The largest kite symbolizes the father. It flies from the top of the pole and may be up to 6 m (20 ft) long.

These red marks represent fish scales.

IRIS LEAVES
The Japanese believe that iris leaves can drive away evil influences. On Kodomono-hi, boys often bathe with the leaves of the plant to protect them from illness and to make them strong.

こどもの日

"My carp's mouth is so big, that if it was real, it could swallow somebody's head!"

"I put this kimono on for the festival. It's quite tight around the chest and I'm happy that I don't have to wear it everyday."

"This is how we write Kodomono-hi in Japanese. My mother wrote this for me and I traced it, because it's quite difficult to write. I help my mother to get my carp streamers ready, but I am really too small to put them on a pole. The pole has to be very tall for the carps to fly in the wind. My carp is blue and it was given to me when I was born. I think I'll fly it until I'm 15. My favourite part of Kodomono-hi is eating the tasty rice cakes."

"My grandparents bought me my Samurai doll when I was a baby. One day I will be strong like the Samurai."

Kazu's Samurai warrior doll

This Samurai warrior doll has a silk costume and gold painted paper armour.

WARRIOR DOLLS
At birth, Japanese boys are given a set of Samurai dolls. The Samurai were courageous Japanese warriors, and the dolls show that the boy will also be strong and fearless. On Kodomono-hi, families with sons arrange a display of their Samurai warrior dolls on a set of steps. The warrior's armour and weapons are also displayed.

SAKE BOTTLES
Japanese rice wine is called *sake*. It is usually served in ceramic bottles and can be drunk hot or cold. On the evening of a boy's first Kodomono-hi, his family and relatives get together at home. They enjoy a splendid meal and drink *sake* to celebrate the new baby.

Ceramic *sake* bottle

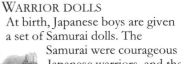

Sasadango are bean paste dumplings wrapped in bamboo leaves.

TASTY SNACKS
Rice cakes called *chimaki* are traditionally eaten throughout Japan on Kodomono-hi. The rice cakes are cone shaped and wrapped in a bamboo leaf. A similar snack, called sasadango, may also be eaten in some areas of northern Japan.

The oak leaves are inedible, but the rice cakes are tasty.

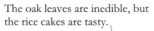

Kashiwa mochi

KASHIWA MOCHI
These leafy snacks are traditionally eaten during Kodomono-hi. *Kashiwa* is an oak leaf, in which the *mochi* (rice cake) is wrapped. Kazu and his family offer these rice cakes to the Samurai warrior dolls before they eat them.

Rice cakes

Esala Perahera

FIFTEEN-YEAR-OLD NISHANTHA lives in Sri Lanka and is a dancer in the magnificent Buddhist festival of Esala Perahera, which takes place each year in August. Over 100 elephants and a myriad of dancers, acrobats, drummers, and flame throwers, take to the streets in the town of Kandy. At the centre of these majestic celebrations is the country's most sacred possession, the Tooth Relic of Lord Buddha, which is paraded throughout the town on the back of a grand old elephant. The festival lasts for ten nights, increasing in size and grandeur until it reaches its climax on the night of the full moon.

MALIGAWA TUSKER

The temple elephant, or *Maligawa Tusker*, leads the procession on the final and most splendid night of the festival. This enormous elephant with magnificent tusks sets out from the *Dalada Maligawa* with a replica of Buddha's sacred Tooth Relic in a golden casket on its back. Attendants lay a white linen cloth in front of the elephant's path so that its feet do not touch the ground, and hold a protective canopy over the casket.

The Esala Perahera takes place in the rainy season, when tropical fruits such as these are in abundance.

Banana

Pineapple

Papaya

During the month of Esala, these *Cassia fistula* trees are in full bloom.

SELLING SNACKS

People travel from all over Sri Lanka to watch the Esala Perahera. They line the streets of Kandy in their thousands. Street sellers move among the waiting crowds selling tasty snacks to hungry families who may wait for hours for the festivities to begin.

Many elephants take part in the procession. Some wear costumes adorned with tiny electric bulbs.

VES DANCERS

Many different groups of dancers take part in the festival. The most important are the *Ves* dancers. In their elaborate handmade costumes of heavy silver headdresses, intricate beaded breastplates, carved silver belts, and huge ankle bells, they look just like armoured warriors. These acrobatic dancers are said to model their dress upon that of the gods.

The *Ves* dancers are a striking sight as they dance through the streets.

Hundreds of golden ornaments decorate the elephant's red velvet costume.

AJIT THE SAVARAN DANCER

Nishantha and his friend, Ajit, both wear simple costumes to show that they are Low Country Dancers. Many festival dancers take their names from the objects or musical instruments that they carry. Ajit, for example, is a *savaran*, or pom pom, dancer. As he dances he shakes his *savaran* and shuffles his feet, both in time with the beat of the drums.

"I start by keeping my arms down, and I shake my savaran to the beat of the drums."

"Then I shake them to my right ..."

"And then to my left."

"I cross my savaran over my head, I stamp my feet and I start all over again."

ඇසළ පෙරහැර

"I have written Esala Perahera in Sinahalese, the language of Sri Lanka. Esala is the time of year and Perahera means procession. I am a *Pantheru* (tambourine) dancer in the festival. My dream is to become a *Ves* dancer, which is the highest point that a dancer can reach. I am not scared that the elephants will stand on my feet when I dance, because I don't stand too near them. I am happy when the festival starts, but I am sad when it is all over."

Samaraja the elephant is four years old and is part of the procession from the *Dalada Maligawa*.

"*My* dhoti (cloth) is four metres (13 ft) long."

"*I wrap my* dhoti *around my body, bring it up between my legs and tuck it in at the top*."

DALADA MALIGAWA

Buddha

The Temple of the Tooth, or *Dalada Maligawa*, was built especially to house the Buddha's Tooth Relic. It is at this elaborate temple with its gilded roof that the festival begins. On the sixth night, *peraheras*, or processions, set out from each of Kandy's four shrines, or *devales*, and make their way

Dalada Maligawa

towards the *Dalada Maligawa*. The four shrines are dedicated to the gods who protect Sri Lanka.

Natha *devale*

NATHA

Maitreya

The entourage from the Natha shrine follows directly behind the one from the *Dalada Maligawa*. Natha is identified with Maitreya, the Buddha-to-be. Each elephant in this procession is dressed in robes of yellow velvet embroidered with images of the god Natha.

VISHNU

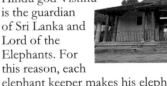
Vishnu

Vishnu *devale*

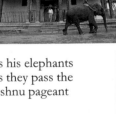

For Buddhists, the Hindu god Vishnu is the guardian of Sri Lanka and Lord of the Elephants. For this reason, each elephant keeper makes his elephants bow down in prayer as they pass the Vishnu shrine. The Vishnu pageant is dressed all in blue.

Kataragama *devale*

KATARAGAMA

Kataragama

The god of war and victory, Kataragama (or Skanda) is the defender of Sri Lanka. On the morning after the last *perahera*, Kataragama's sword is cleansed in a tradition called the "water cutting" ceremony and the Tooth Relic is returned to the *Dalada Maligawa*.

PATTINI

Pattini

Pattini *devale*

The goddess Pattini joins the procession last. She represents fertility and health and each of her elephants is dressed in golden cloaks. The Pattini procession is the only one to include women; their dances tell stories of health and village life.

Raksha Bandhan

LIKE MILLIONS OF brothers and sisters throughout northern India, ten-year-old Suman and her younger brother Manoj celebrate their love for each other every year in a festival called Raksha Bandhan, which takes place in August. The sister ties a bracelet of woven threads, called a *rakhi*, around her brother's wrist. In return, he vows to protect her. This tradition dates back more than 500 years, when sisters tied *rakhis* on their brothers' wrist to protect them on the battlefield.

MORNING PRAYERS
On the morning of Raksha Bandhan, Suman and Manoj begin the day by praying at their family shrine. Their parents perform a small prayer ceremony, called a *puja*. Suman and Manoj also pray at school every day. Here, they are honouring the god Ganesh and the goddess Lakshmi. Ganesh is the god of wisdom and is recognized by his elephant head. Lakshmi is the goddess of wealth and prosperity.

PERFORMING *PUJA*
After morning prayers, sisters perform the Raksha Bandhan *puja*. Suman sits opposite her brother, with a tray placed between them.

TRAY OF DELIGHTS
For the Raksha Bandhan ceremony, sweets, *rakhis*, an oil lamp, and some orange turmeric powder are all placed on a stainless steel tray.

Hindus light an oil lamp for most ceremonies.

Suman's homemade *rakhis*

In the past, saffron was used for the *tilak*. Today, however, sisters use turmeric powder because it is cheaper.

Pieces of *laddu*

"First, I say a prayer. Then I put a tilak on Manoj's forehead, and a grain of rice on top of the tilak."

"I tie the rakhi on my brother's wrist. The pretty decoration must be on top."

BAND OF PROTECTION
Manoj will wear his *rakhi* until it frays and falls off. Some *rakhis* can last for up to four weeks.

1 Suman blesses her brother with a holy mark, called a *tilak*. The *tilak* is a symbol of success.

2 When Suman ties the bracelet on her brother's right wrist, he promises to protect her.

"I like laddu, but my favourite sweet is gulab jamun."

"With the two rupees that Manoj has given me, I shall buy some bangles and some jewellery for my nose."

SWEET MARKET
The giving of sweets is part of every Indian festival. During Raksha Bandhan, siblings offer each other pieces of *laddu, gulab jamun*, and *barfi*. These can be made at home or bought from shops such as this one.

3 The siblings then exchange a piece of Indian sweet. Suman and Manoj give each other some *laddu*.

4 At the end of the ceremony, the brother gives the sister a gift. Manoj gives Suman two rupees.

These delicious sweets contain rice or coconut milk.

रक्षा बन्धन

"On Raksha Bandhan, we'll have a bath and put on new clothes."

"I think Manoj will look after me when I'm big."

"Raksha means 'protection' and Bandhan means 'bond'. I have written this in Hindi, which is the language that I speak. To me, the best bit of Raksha Bandhan is that I'll tie a *rakhi* on my brother's wrist and I'll give him a *laddu* to eat. I have another baby brother and sister. I give my baby brother a *rakhi*, too. I like the very shiny gold *rakhis*, but I wouldn't know how to make one like that. I just make one with paper and a few colourful *bindis*. First thing in the morning on Raksha Bandhan, we say our prayers. When I pray, I pray that my brothers and sisters remain safe and that nothing will happen to them."

"After I have given my brother the rakhi, *we'll all go out and play."*

"Manoj keeps my two rupees safe in his pocket."

"I tie the threads to my toe to keep them in place."

Tiny coloured plastic discs called *bindis* make the *rakhi* sparkle.

HOMEMADE *RAKHIS*
Usually Suman's father buys *rakhis* for Suman to give, but this year, she is making her own. She begins by carefully weaving the threads together. Then she decorates it with flower shapes cut from yellow paper and a few sparkling *bindis*.

RAKHIS FOR SALE
As the festival of Raksha Bandhan approaches, glittering *rakhis* fill the shop fronts and market stalls. There are hundreds of different types of *rakhi* to choose from. Some are scented, because they are decorated with tiny pieces of sandalwood, others sparkle as they catch the bright shop lights.

35

Dalia in her prayer clothes

Eid ul-Fitr

DALIA IS ELEVEN YEARS OLD and lives in Jordan. Dalia and her family are Muslims. Each year during the ninth lunar month, called Ramadan, Muslims avoid food and drink between sunrise and sunset. They celebrate the end of this period of fasting with Eid ul-Fitr, a joyous festival of feasting that lasts for three days. At Eid, Muslims eat celebratory meals, give food to the poor, visit relations and friends, and exchange gifts and cards.

According to the Qur'an, only your hands and your face can show during prayer; the rest of your body must be covered.

Muslims always take off their shoes before they enter the mosque or pray.

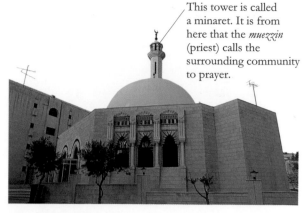

This tower is called a minaret. It is from here that the *muezzin* (priest) calls the surrounding community to prayer.

DALIA'S MOSQUE
Most Muslim women pray at home, but on the first day of Eid, Dalia and the rest of her family attend special prayers at their local mosque. Dalia and her mother have to enter the mosque through a different entrance to her father and her brother, Hasan.

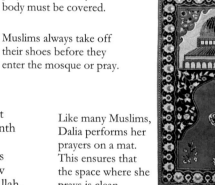

Like many Muslims, Dalia performs her prayers on a mat. This ensures that the space where she prays is clean.

CLOTHES FOR PRAYING
Muslims give thanks to Allah at Eid for his help during the month of fasting. Dalia wears a white gown over her everyday clothes when she prays. This is to show that everyone is equal before Allah.

HOLY MECCA
For Muslims, the most sacred city in the world is Mecca. Situated in Saudi Arabia in the heart of the Middle East, Mecca is where the prophet Mohammad was born. Muslims have to face Mecca when they pray, and if they can, every Muslim must make the pilgrimage to Mecca at least once during their lifetime.

PRAYERS
An announcement from the mosque calls Muslims to prayer, or *salah*. They normally pray five times a day, but on Eid day, there is also a special Eid prayer that is performed after sunset, either at a mosque or in a clean open yard.

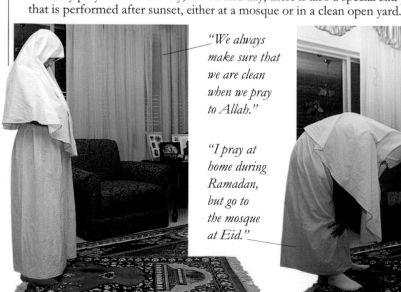

"We always make sure that we are clean when we pray to Allah."

"I pray at home during Ramadan, but go to the mosque at Eid."

"Praying helps me to avoid thinking about food."

1 Dalia changes into her prayer clothes and rolls out her prayer mat. She faces Mecca and stands upright to show that she must be upright and well behaved before Allah.

2 Dalia bows down in her second position to show respect and reverence for Allah. She recites verses from the Qur'an, repeating Allah's name at the same time.

3 For the final position, Dalia performs prostration to represent complete submission to Allah. Her knees, feet, hands, and face must all touch the prayer mat.

"Fasting helps us to remember the poor, who never have food and are always hungry."

"I am so excited and happy when Eid comes, because we go to visit my cousins and grandparents and they give us presents and money."

"When people visit during Eid, we give them candy, chocolates that my mother makes, and ma'moul."

"We get new clothes for Eid, and these are my first pair of high heeled shoes."

"This is the Arabic word Eid ul-Fitr, which means 'breaking of the fast'. For the month of Ramadan, we don't eat or drink anything between sunrise and sunset. Ramadan ends on the morning after we have seen the new moon in the sky, and this is the first day of Eid. We get up before sunrise, have a bath, and put on new clothes. Then we go to the mosque and pray until the sun has risen. After that, we go home and eat what we want for breakfast. I think that everyone feels very happy at Eid."

"When my alarm clock goes off on the morning of Eid, it says the words 'Allah o Akbar' (Allah the Greatest). These are the words that are called from the mosque."

DALIA'S HOUSE
This is Dalia's house in Amman, the capital of Jordan, where she lives with her family. At Eid, Dalia's family sometimes invites poor people to their house, so that they can share their food. Ramadan and Eid ul-Fitr are a time for remembering people in need.

BREAK FAST, BREAKFAST
The word breakfast literally means 'to break your fast'. On the morning of Eid ul-Fitr, Dalia and her family return home from the mosque to enjoy the freedom of eating a large breakfast. This Eid, Dalia ate *labaneh* with bread and thyme, which is a herb.

Dates

DATES AND WATER
The fast of Ramadan is called *sawm*, and it shows Muslims that they can enjoy the good things in life, but not over-indulge in them. Muslims break their fast each evening by eating a few dates and drinking a glass of water, following in the tradition of Prophet Mohammad.

Water

Money box

Eid card

EID SNACKS
Dalia helps her mother to make small biscuits called *ma'moul* for Eid. She mixes semolina, dates, and pistachio nuts and presses the dough into a mould. This gives the biscuits their distinctive shape.

Wooden mould

"For Eid, all our relatives give us gifts of money. I put all the money in this big money box. It is so heavy!"

People send special cards at Eid.

Ma'moul

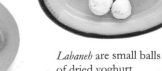

Labaneh are small balls of dried yoghurt.

Autumn

Autumn festivals share common themes of harvest and remembrance. As the nights get longer, children eagerly await their favourite festival by making fancy dress costumes and masks, and helping to prepare harvest foods.

Petal cross

Witch

TRUNG THU

• Date: 15th day of the eighth lunar month
• Place: Vietnam
• This mid-autumn festival celebrates the beauty of the October full moon. The moon is considered especially important at this time of year because its brightness helps to banish the darkness of the long nights.

HALLOWE'EN

• Date: 31 October   • Origin: northern Europe
• All Saints' Day takes place on 1 November and the evening before is called All Hallows' Eve. On this day, ancient cultures believed that the souls of the dead, and supernatural beings such as ghosts and witches visited the Earth. People lit bonfires and dressed up in spooky costumes to drive away the evil spirits.

DAY OF THE DEAD

• Date: 1 and 2 November • Religion: Christian
• For many Mexicans, this festival provides a link between the dead and the living. Mexicans build altars, visit cemeteries, and pray to the souls of their dead ancestors and relatives to return to the land of the living for just one night.

THANKSGIVING

• Date: November • Place: North America
• Thanksgiving is the biggest celebration in North America and marks the arrival of the first English settlers there in 1620. Many settlers died during their first winter. Those who survived learned how to hunt food and plant crops from the local American Indians, and gave thanks to God when they gathered in an excellent harvest the next year.

These are the children who you will be meeting in this section of the book. They all take part in festivals that occur during the autumn months in their country.

Vân from Vietnam   Alex from Canada   Diego from Mexico   Luke from the United States

Trung Thu

VAN IS TWELVE YEARS OLD and lives in Vietnam. Each year, on the 15th day of the eighth lunar month, she joins hordes of other children who go out into the streets with glowing lanterns to enjoy Trung Thu. This mid-autumn festival celebrates the beauty of the moon, which is brighter and whiter than at any other time of the year. The festival involves a family gathering where parents spoil their children with treats and tasty moon cakes.

"The moon is bright and full and you can count so many stars."

LANTERN BUYING
On the day of the festival, Vân goes with her parents to buy a star lantern from the market. The lanterns represent the brightness of the moon as they light up the dark night.

Candles make the lanterns glow.

HANG MA STREET
Bursting with vibrant colours, this narrow street in the centre of Hanoi sells beautiful decorations especially for Trung Thu. The stalls are laden with shiny red lanterns, multi-coloured masks, water pistols, and many other toys. On the days leading up to the festival, the street is bustling with families desperate to buy a lantern for Trung Thu.

Moon mask

Pig mask

MASK STALL
Vân and her friends enjoy wearing masks on Trung Thu. In the past, children made their own masks, but today they buy them. Colourful stalls are dotted all around Hang Ma street, which sell a wonderful variety of plastic and papier mâché masks.

Demon mask

LAKE AND BOAT
During Trung Thu, some children head for Hanoi's Hoan Kiem lake, where they sail little handmade boats made from scrap metal.

Quân is 10 years old.

40

Trung Thu

"On Trung Thu, the moon looks like a yellow ball, full and beautiful. My mother buys me moon cakes and I arrange them on a tray with some fruit. We eat these on the terrace. Then I put a candle inside my star lantern, light it, and go outside to meet my friends and follow the processions through the streets."

"The frame is made from bamboo with plastic stretched across it."

"We sing songs about star lanterns. These are my favourite lanterns."

Vân

Ha is eight years old.

Incense sticks

MOON CAKE STALL .
On almost every street corner, there are stalls selling fish- and flower-shaped moon cakes. Moon cakes are a traditional part of the Trung Thu festivities and come in two varieties. *Bánh deo* is unbaked, white and sticky and *bánh nuong* is brown and baked. Moon cakes contain unusual sweet fillings, such as sugar with meat or egg.

Moon cakes

"I prefer the baked moon cakes, bánh nuong. *I only like the big fish-shaped cake."*

DEAD RELATIVES
Trung Thu is also a time for people to remember their relatives who have died. Vân prays for her grandfather as she lights sweet smelling incense and burns bundles of fake Vietnamese money in his memory. Money signifies good luck, which is carried up to the relatives in the burning smoke.

Fake Vietnamese money

UNICORN DANCERS
The Trung Thu festivities often include unicorn dancers. The dancers weave their way through the crowded streets to the accompaniment of drums and cymbals. This tradition originated in China.

Hallowe'en

ALEX IS TEN YEARS OLD and lives in Canada. This year, his neighbour Megan has invited him to a party to celebrate Hallowe'en. Hallowe'en is an ancient festival that takes place on the last night of October, when it was once believed that witches and spirits returned to Earth. Children have great fun decorating their houses and dressing up in different disguises. As night falls, they go from door to door, frightening their neighbours and saying "trick or treat".

Glowing pumpkins lit by candles and carved with smiles are placed in windows to ward off evil spirits.

Alex

HOUSE OF HORROR
Transforming the house into a place of horror is part of the festive fun. The Hallowe'en display in Alex's front garden was so effective that children from the local school came especially to see it.

An open coffin with a cobweb-tangled skeleton provides a spooky welcome to Alex's house.

GRASSY GRAVES
Two terrifying figures lie on the lawn outside Alex's house, making his garden look like a graveyard. Alex's mother has stuffed white sheets with autumn leaves and used gruesome masks for their faces. She even managed to find paving slabs for gravestones!

"My mom bought both our costumes from a shop. Sometimes we make them."

WITCH WITCH
At the party, Alex and his friends play "Witch, Witch", a game invented by his neighbour. Each child takes a turn at being the witch, while the other children walk around in a circle and sing a Hallowe'en rhyme.

Piñata is a birthday game from Mexico. Megan's mother decided to play it at Megan's Hallowe'en birthday party, and made a *piñata* in the shape of a ghost.

"Last year I dressed up as the cartoon character Bugs Bunny."

TEETH TRICKS
Bobbing and catching apples is a traditional Hallowe'en game. Apples float in a bucket of water or hang from a tree. With their hands behind their backs, the players must capture the apples with their teeth.

SMASH THE *PINATA*
A *piñata* is a papier mâché figure filled with sweets. Using a stick, each child takes it in turn to hit the figure until it breaks. As the sweets fall from the smashed *piñata*, the children scramble for their share of the treasure!

"These pumpkin buckets are good for trick or treating because we can store our treats in them."

"My brother Ryan loves the show Power Rangers. *He is dressed up as the character Adam, the Ninja frog."*

Hallowe'en

"This is a scary time of year. My neighbour Megan is having a Hallowe'en party. I am going as the Giant Hamster from the *Goosebumps* books. He is ugly with big teeth and has grown huge and evil after eating some Monster Blood. At Megan's party we'll play my favourite game, which is apple bobbing. When we go trick or treating, people always give us treats. My favourite treats are suckers."

The Giant Hamster features in the "Monster Blood 2" book of the *Goosebumps* series.

Ryan is five years old.

Trick or treat sweets

TRICK OR TREAT
Transformed by masks and scary costumes, children go from house to house on Hallowe'en night, calling "trick or treat". This tradition comes from the Celtic belief that the spirits would use their powers against people who failed to honour them at the New Year festivities. Today, most children get treats, such as sweets or crisps, and do not play mischievous tricks.

Skull torch

In Canada and the US, trick or treaters often carry UNICEF donation boxes, so that people can give money to help children all around the world.

ANCIENT FESTIVAL
Hallowe'en has its roots in an ancient Celtic festival called Samhain. Samhain marked the end of summer and was held on the 31 October. Like today's Hallowe'en, it was seen as a scary time, when evil spirits roamed the Earth causing mischief.

Witches on broomsticks are said to fill the skies at Hallowe'en.

CLEVER DISGUISES
Children love dressing up in different disguises at Hallowe'en. Witches and ghosts reflect the spooky origins of the festival, but cats, princesses, and cartoon characters are also popular costumes choices.

Day of the Dead

Diego

EIGHT-YEAR-OLD DIEGO lives in a tiny village in eastern Mexico. Every year on 1 November, he and his family, together with families throughout Mexico, celebrate the Day of the Dead. During this festival, they pray to the souls of their dead relatives so that they will return to the land of the living for just one night. They build altars in their homes and in cemeteries, and decorate them with cooked foods, candles, sugar skulls, and colourful flowers to welcome back the dead.

"I cut the pink flowers from our field and put them on the altar."

SUGAR SKULLS
In the days leading up to the festival, market stalls throughout Mexico are filled with elaborate models of skulls, coffins, and skeletons. The models are made entirely from sugar and water. People buy these sweets to place on their altars.

The names of the dead relatives are written in icing sugar on the sugar skulls.

"My brother Juan is holding a sugar cross, which is for los angelitos."

FOOD OF THE DEAD
Families prepare favourite dishes to welcome the souls of their dead relatives back to earth. They cook large quantities of food so that living members of the family can also enjoy the feast. Tiny sugar-crafted models of traditional dishes adorn many of the altars.

These *enchiladas* are made out of sugar. Real *enchiladas* are thin pancakes filled with meat.

Mexicans make a special bread for this festival. It is called *pan de muerto* (bread of the dead) and is shaped like a person.

Sugar-crafted model of crispy *tacos*

There are many different types of skull to choose from.

FESTIVAL FLOWERS
Altars to the dead must be decorated with flowers. During the festival, flower stalls sell many different kinds of brightly coloured flowers. The most popular is the marigold, or *zempasuchitl*, which is the traditional flower of the dead.

Orange marigolds and purple orchids are among the colourful variety of flowers found in the market.

Bright red flowers decorate some of the altars.

Juan is two years old.

44

El dia de los muertos

"I have written 'The Day of the Dead' in Spanish. We remember our family on this festival, so we don't get sad. I helped my grandmother make food for the *angelitos*. We made them fish soup, but we didn't put chilli in it, or the *angelitos* would get burned. Babies don't like chillies. For the grown-ups' altar, I helped my uncle to put the marigold petals in the shape of a man."

"My brother Doroteo has also helped to cut some flowers."

Diego put this sugar coffin on the altar to *los angelitos.*

BABY ANGELS
The morning of the festival is dedicated to *los angelitos* (little angels), the children who have died. Families prepare special food for them, without chilli or other spices. They place a dish and a candle on the altar, together with some fruit and other food that the children would have liked.

Tamale is corn dough wrapped in corn husks and steamed.

Cheese soup with corn bread

"I would like to have bananas and mangoes on my altar."

GROWN UP ALTARS
In the afternoon, families welcome the souls of older family members. They prepare different, spicier foods for the adults and may put a bottle of a Mexican alcohol called tequila on the altar.

Spicy fish curry for the adults.

"We used marigold petals to decorate the grown ups' altar."

VISITING THE CEMETERY
The night before the festival, families visit the cemeteries where their relatives are buried to tidy up the graves. Diego's parents think he is too young to go to the cemetery, but he does help to cut some flowers for decorating the tombs.

CEMETERY BY CANDLELIGHT
Illuminated by candles, the graves appear to twinkle in the night. A candle is bought for each soul and lit to help it find its way back to the land of the living. Some families spend the entire night beside their relative's grave, but Diego's family only stay until about 8 or 9 pm, because they live a long way from the cemetery.

Doroteo is five years old.

Candles light up the darkness of the cemetery.

Thanksgiving

LUKE IS SIX YEARS OLD and lives in Bronxville, USA. Each year, on the fourth Thursday in November, his whole family gets together to share a wonderful feast, celebrating the day of Thanksgiving. This family event is one of the most important festivals in North America. It marks the early settlers' first harvest, nearly 400 years ago, when they gave thanks to God for surviving their first year in this new land.

"Grace is my little sister and Faith and Sam are my cousins."

Sam is five years old.

"We dress up in our best clothes on Thanksgiving."

NANA'S HOUSE
On Thanksgiving Day, families are usually invited to one family member's house for a meal. Luke's grandmother, Nancy, always holds the gathering at her home in Yonkers. Yonkers is close to Bronxville, where Luke lives.

FAMILY MEAL
Each member of Luke's family contributes to the Thanksgiving celebration by preparing a dish for the huge feast. The table is beautifully laid for this special occasion, with the best crockery, a tablecloth, and candles. When the food is placed on the table and everyone is seated, the family recites a prayer, thanking God for the plentiful food.

Bob, Luke's father

Aunt Franny

Nana

Uncle Randy

Uncle Timothy

Faith

Allison, Luke's mother

Cousin Sam

Grace

Uncle John

Luke and his family eat their Thanksgiving meal in the evening.

DELICIOUS DISHES
The Thanksgiving meal is abundant with autumn fruits and vegetables, such as pumpkin, potatoes, apples, and cranberries. However, the feast is not complete without turkey, which is roasted and served with cranberry sauce. Turkey is traditionally eaten on Thanksgiving because the early settlers in America had to catch wild turkeys. Pumpkins were also a significant part of the early settlers' diet, both as a vegetable and a dessert. Today they are sweetened with sugar and served in pies.

Delicious pies, such as apple, pecan, and pumpkin are served for dessert at the Thanksgiving meal.

Roast turkey

Homemade cranberry sauce

Apple pie

Pecan pie

Pumpkin pie

Mashed sweet potato

"My favourite pie is apple pie."

Faith is seven
years old.

Luke

Grace is
three years old.

THANKSGIVING

"Thanksgiving is when we give thanks for everything
we've got. I like it that my cousins come. We don't
get presents, we just play. I don't really like meat, so I
don't eat the turkey, but I do help my mom to make
the stuffing for the turkey. I put all of the ingredients
in a bowl and then I mix it around."

PLAYING GAMES

The part of Thanksgiving that most children
like best is the opportunity to play with other
members of their family. Here, Luke is playing
the board game Monopoly with his cousins.
Luke and his eldest cousin, Faith, are showing
their younger siblings how to play.

Luke drew this picture
of a turkey for his
mother and father.

DECORATING THE HOUSE

Many families decorate their houses for Thanksgiving
using table decorations and drawings. Luke has a
candle with cranberries made of wax and a
turkey-shaped candleholder. At school,
Luke made a model of a turkey. He
used a brown paper bag for its body
and coloured feathers for its wings.

*"I coloured my
turkey brown and
stuck tan, brown,
orange, and black
feathers on it."*

THE THANKSGIVING STORY

This book belongs to Luke and tells
the story of how Thanksgiving Day
began. In 1621, when the early
settlers arrived in America from
England, they suffered a winter of
starvation. The following harvest was
good and they gave thanks for their
bountiful crops with a great feast.

Winter

Winter festivals share common themes of light and warmth. Children look forward to lighting candles and filling their houses with colourful, festive decorations to brighten up the long, dark days of winter.

Stocking

Hanukkiya

DIWALI

- Date: October / November • Religion: Hindu
- This festival is dedicated to Lakshmi, the goddess of prosperity, and celebrates the return from exile of Lord Rama, hero of the epic Ramayana. Clay lamps called *diye* were lit to illuminate Rama and Sita's return to their kingdom, where they were welcomed as the new rulers.

ST. LUCIA

- Date: 13 December • Religion: Christian
- St. Lucia was an early Christian martyr and the patron saint of light and brightness. She always wore a crown of candles on her head. St. Lucia's Day falls in the middle of winter and is meant to brighten up the long, dark days.

HANUKKAH

- Date: December • Religion: Jewish
- In 165 BC, a small group of Jews called the Maccabees recaptured Jerusalem from the Syrian King Antiochus IV. After cleaning the temple, they could only find enough oil to light the *Hanukkiya* for one day. Miraculously, the oil lasted for eight days.

ST. NICHOLAS

- Date: 6 December • Religion: Christian
- This festival marks the birthday of St. Nicholas, a Catholic bishop who was especially kind to children. Unlike the jolly fat Santa Claus who visits children with gifts at Christmas, St. Nicholas is portrayed as a tall, thin man.

CHRISTMAS

- Date: 25 December – early January
- Religion: Christian
- Christmas is the time when Christians all over the world celebrate the birth of Jesus Christ. Christians believe that Jesus was no ordinary baby, but instead was the Son of God, sent to spread the word of God.

EPIPHANY

- Date: 6 January • Religion: Christian
- The word epiphany comes from the Greek word *epiphaneia*, which means "appearance". This festival celebrates the arrival of the Three Kings, or Wise Men, in Bethlehem to worship the baby Jesus.

These are the children who you will be meeting in this section of the book. They all take part in festivals that occur during the winter months in their country.

Sonu from India   Karin from Sweden   Isabel from the United States   Matús from Slovakia   Maria from Germany   Alejandra from Spain

Diwali

ELEVEN-YEAR-OLD SONU lives in northern India. Each autumn, just before the new moon, when the sky is at its darkest, Sonu celebrates Diwali, the magnificent festival of lights. Houses all over India twinkle with tiny lights from clay lamps called *diye* (singular *diya*), which are lit to welcome the Hindu god Rama. On this day thousands of years ago, Rama returned to reclaim his kingdom after 14 years in exile. People also light *diye* in the hope that Lakshmi, the goddess of prosperity, will visit their homes. Diwali lasts for two days – on the second night, families pray and feast and set off fireworks to ward off evil.

TWINKLING HOUSES
During Diwali, houses throughout India are adorned with tiny lamps, called *diye*. After prayers, children place the lamps in every corner of the house.

STALLS SELLING FIREWORKS
Two days before Diwali, people clean their houses thoroughly and buy supplies for the festivities. Attractive stalls selling fireworks and sweets line the streets of every Indian town. Many of the fireworks have images of the goddess Lakshmi emblazoned on them.

Fireworks

Fireworks

PUFFED RICE STALL
Piles of small rice puffs, called *khil*, are sold everywhere during Diwali. Families buy *khil* by the kilogram. They offer them to Lakshmi, and to friends and relatives they visit during Diwali.

GIVING GIFTS
Neighbours and friends visit each other during Diwali, bearing gifts. They exchange traditional Indian coconut sweets, or small sugar discs, called *patashe*. A more recent custom is to send Diwali greeting cards.

Box of Indian sweets

This Diwali greeting card has a picture of the god Ganesh on it.

Sugar discs called *patashe*

"My grandfather lights the first diya.*"*

"We all help to light the other diye*, which must be lit from the first* diya*. Then we put them around the house."*

PREPARING WICKS
The first day of Diwali is called Choti (little) Diwali. One *diya* is lit on this day. Sonu's mother and elder sister make the wicks for the clay *diye* by entwining small pieces of cotton together to form thin strips. Then they place the wicks in the lamps.

The clay *diye* give off a warm glow when lit.

The wicks float in oil.

Mustard oil keeps the wick alight.

WELCOMING *RANGOLI*
For Diwali, Sonu and his mother use rice flour to create a pattern called *rangoli* in front of their household shrine. *Rangoli* adorns the floors in all Hindu houses during festivals to welcome visitors.

At least 50 *diye* light up every house.

"It takes about 20 minutes to light all the diye.*"*

"We pray to Lakshmi that we will live a long and happy life."

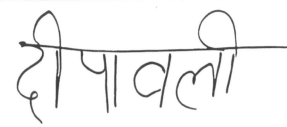

"The word Diwali comes from the Hindi word Deepavali, which I have written here. Deepavali means 'row of lights'. Today is Diwali and it is also my birthday, which is very lucky. On Diwali, we wear clean clothes or new clothes. In the evening we pray to Lakshmi and then we touch our elders' feet to show our respect for them. We offer sweets to Lakshmi, and after the prayers, we share sweets among ourselves."

Lakshmi

NEW YEAR, NEW BOOKS

For businessmen, Diwali marks the beginning of a new financial year. Old account books are closed and new ones are bought. This account book stall in Rajasthan sells books by their weight. As a symbol of good luck, each book contains a picture of Lakshmi.

FAMILY PUJA

Families get together to celebrate Diwali and to perform a prayer, or *puja*, in honour of Lakshmi. Sonu and his family decorate their shrine with flower garlands and make offerings of sweets, such as *khil* and *patashe*. The head of the household recites prayers and then blesses everyone in the family. After the ceremony, the family light the *diye*.

Saraswathi   Ganesh

DIFFERENT GODS

Although Diwali is dedicated to the goddess Lakshmi, many people also pray to Ganesh, the god of wisdom and good luck. Ganesh is easily recognized by his elephant head. On Diwali, Sonu also worships Saraswathi, the goddess of knowledge.

Fireworks

"We light the diye after sunset. This is usually between 7 and 7.30 in the evening."

SONU WITH FIREWORKS

For most children, the best part of the Diwali celebrations is setting off fireworks. After praying, Sonu and his siblings take their fireworks out into the courtyard. Sonu likes sparklers and rockets, but his favourite fireworks are crackers because of the noise they make.

Hanukkah

SEVEN-YEAR-OLD ISABEL comes from New York City, USA. She and her family are Jewish and each year, on the 25th day of the Jewish month of *Kislev* (usually around December), they celebrate Hanukkah, the festival of lights. Hanukkah lasts for eight days and features an eight-branched candlestick, which Jews use to remind them of the miracle that happened when the Temple of Jerusalem was re-captured and cleansed, more than 2,000 years ago.

ISABEL'S HOMEMADE *HANUKKIYA*
This year, Isabel has made her own *hanukkiya* out of clay. Using a wooden stick for the base, she moulded nine strips of moist clay into candlestick holders. Once the clay had dried, she painted it.

Candles for the *hanukkiya*

Michael is seven years old.

THE FAMILY *HANUKKIYA*
This elaborate candlestick is called a *hanukkiya*. It holds nine candles, eight of which represent each night of Hanukkah. The ninth candle in the middle is called the *shamash* and is used for lighting the others.

LIGHTING THE *HANUKKIYA*
On the first night of Hanukkah, Isabel uses the *shamash* to light the first candle. Over the next seven nights, she lights a new candle until they all burn together brightly on the last night. The new candle should always be lit first.

The *hanukkiya* is often placed in the window during Hanukkah so that people can see it.

"I always forget how to play dreidl, but my dad is going to show me."

OPENING PRESENTS
Some children receive eight small presents for each night of the festival, but Isabel is given one big present on the first night of Hanukkah. Many people wrap the gifts in blue and white paper, the colours of the Israeli flag.

Isabel's Hanukkah present

PLAYING *DREIDL*
During Hanukkah, Jewish people are encouraged not to work while the candles are alight. Instead, they play traditional games such as *dreidl*. Players spin a four-sided top and receive a pile of chocolate coins if they win. Each side of the top is marked with a Hebrew initial. If *dreidl* is played in Israel, the initials spell out "A great miracle happened here"; if it is played elsewhere, they spell "A great miracle happened there".

Each player spins the top, and depending on which initial the top lands on, the player has to either take all of the coins, take none of the coins, replace half, or take half.

Isabel and Michael are playing for chocolate money, but children also play for raisins or real money.

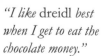

"I like dreidl best when I get to eat the chocolate money."

hanukkah

"At Hanukkah, we light candles in our *hanukkiya*. Actually we have two – one that I made from clay, and the other, real one, which is golden. Last night I watched a tape about Hanukkah and the other day, I called my dad's mom, who told me the story behind it. Hanukkah is one of my favourite festivals. I like making little cards for my mom and dad with 'Happy Hanukkah' on them, and I also make my own *dreidls* out of some paper, tape, and a pencil. Most of all, I love eating the *latkes* that my mom makes."

FAMILY REUNION
Like many festivals, the Hanukkah holiday provides an opportunity for families to get together. Each night, they light candles and recite special blessings before the meal is taken. Isabel's immediate family are Jewish, but they do not pray before their meals or before lighting the *hanukkiya*. Joining them this year for Hanukkah are Isabel's friend Michael and his family, who are visiting from Los Angeles.

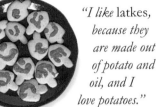

"I like latkes, because they are made out of potato and oil, and I love potatoes."

"My dad loves latkes. Once he ate 10 of them!"

"Bridget is my dog."

"I'm going to buy Bridget something fun for Hanukkah."

FRYING *LATKES*
Isabel's mother prepares the Hanukkah speciality – *latkes*, or potato cakes. She grates some potatoes and an onion and mixes them with flour and eggs. Then she moulds the mixture into small cakes, which are fried in sizzling olive oil. The oil represents the oil which burned miraculously in the temple for eight days.

Isabel

"I only eat sour cream with my latkes."

Latkes are eaten with apple sauce and sour cream.

Apple sauce

Sour cream

"My friend Michael won the last game of dreidl, but I am winning this game."

St. Nicholas

THERE IS ONLY ONE NIGHT of the year when seven-year-old Matús, who lives in Slovakia, looks forward to going to bed. On 5 December, the eve of St. Nicholas Day, he puts a polished boot on his windowsill and quickly goes to sleep, eager for the morning to come. Like children all over Eastern Europe, Matús believes that during this night, St. Nicholas, the patron saint of children, will come and fill good children's boots with treats.

"I woke up very early. It was just getting light, but I could see the sweets sticking out of my boot. I also got a banana and a tangerine."

MEETING ST. NICHOLAS
On the eve of St. Nicholas Day, a person dressed as St. Nicholas came to Matús's house to give him and his sister Zuzi a bag of sweets. However, Matús believes that the real St. Nicholas visits houses only in the middle of the night.

Children always receive two toys: a toy devil to show that they are sometimes naughty and a St. Nicholas toy to show that they are also good.

Devil

St. Nicholas

Mikuláš

"St. Nicholas has a long white beard. He wears red trousers, a red coat, and a bishop's hat. I think he flies to everybody's house and he doesn't have anybody helping him because he is strong. I think he lives in heaven."

This stocking contains a naughty devil. It is one of the decorations in Matús's house.

BOOTS ON WINDOWSILL
Slovakian children take great care in polishing one of their boots for St. Nicholas to fill with treats. Matús and Zuzi place their boots on the bedroom windowsill and leave one of the windows half open so that St. Nicholas can get in.

Delicious sweets and chocolate treats if you are good.

A bag of sweets from St. Nicholas

Coal, potatoes, onions, and devils if you are naughty.

Children use boots instead of shoes so that there is plenty of room for goodies.

Matús decorated his bedroom by drawing a picture of St. Nicholas.

"There were some potatoes and coals in my boot too, because I was bad."

St. Lucia

ON 13 DECEMBER, one of the longest, darkest winter nights in Sweden, the festival of St. Lucia takes place. St. Lucia is the patron saint of light and nine-year-old Karin celebrates this day by lighting a candle in Lucia's honour, eating lussekatt buns, and singing carols. Throughout Sweden, many schools elect a pupil to be St. Lucia. This year, Karin was chosen to lead the St. Lucia procession at her school.

ST. LUCIA PAGEANT
Karin had to dress as St. Lucia to lead the procession at her school. She wore a long white gown with a red sash, and a brass crown with burning candles on her head. A group of her schoolfriends followed behind as her maidens.

The St. Lucia crown is made with sprigs of lingonberry and candles. Lingonberry is an evergreen and symbolizes new life during the bleak winter.

The candles on Karin's crown create the effect of a halo.

Sankta Lucia.

"As I led the St. Lucia day procession at school, my heart was beating hard and fast. I had to keep my head still, as the crown had real candles and the wax dripped onto my hair. The candles in my crown at home use batteries."

In schools, children sing a special carol called "Sancta Lucia".

"To be St. Lucia, I must wear a long white dress with a red sash."

"I tie the red sash around my waist."

It took Karin two hours to make the *lussekatt* buns.

Lussekatt buns

"We have lussekatts for breakfast. They taste good, but I don't like the raisins."

BAKING *LUSSEKATTS*
Traditionally on St. Lucia's Day, Swedish people eat saffron flavoured buns dotted with raisins. These are called *lussekatts*, or Lucia cats. Karin made her own *lussekatts*. She pulled the dough into different shapes before baking it.

Gingerbread biscuits are also eaten on St. Lucia's day.

Christmas

NINE-YEAR-OLD MARIA lives in Stuttgart, Germany. Her favourite celebrations are her birthday and Christmas – a Christian festival to mark the birth of Jesus Christ. On 24 December, which is Christmas Eve, Maria, her sister, and children throughout Germany go to church. They believe that while they are there, Christkind (baby Christ) visits their homes to deliver gifts. Every German household has a green fir tree at Christmas. Maria decorates her tree with glittering hearts.

NATIVITY SCENE
Christians believe that Jesus was born in a stable nearly 2,000 years ago, in the town of Bethlehem. An Angel visited shepherds in the fields outside Bethlehem to tell them about Jesus' birth and the shepherds went to visit him. Three Wise Men from the east followed a bright star to where Jesus lay, and gave him gifts of gold, frankincense, and myrrh. This event is called the Nativity.

"We bought our tree at the Christmas market in Stuttgart."

"I decorated half of the tree and my sister decorated the other half."

CAROL SINGERS
Carols are joyous hymns, sung especially at Christmas. They explain the Christmas story. Many carols are hundreds of years old. Maria and her sister Anna love singing carols – in church, at school, and at home.

CHURCH SERVICES
Many churches hold special services at Christmas to celebrate the birth of Jesus. Part of the service can be a Nativity play, in which children act out the scene at Bethlehem. This year Maria dressed up as one of the Angels who tells the shepherds about Jesus' birth.

"I have drawn a picture of my local church, which is where we perform the play."

"This is the music for one of my favourite carols, 'Silent Night'. I sing a lot in my Nativity play."

"We sing a special song to Christkind before we open our presents."

CHRISTMAS CARDS
The first commercially printed Christmas cards were made in England in 1843. Today, Christians all over the world send cards at Christmas as a way of keeping in touch with family and friends.

Gingerbread heart

FAMILY FEAST
Christmas Day is traditionally a time for families and friends to get together, and eat hot, rich foods to drive away thoughts of the cold, dark winter. Germany is famous for its festive treats of spiced biscuits and cakes, such as *stollen* and gingerbread. Maria's family eat goose for their main meal, followed by homemade cookies which they bake with almonds, coconuts, and sugar.

Stollen

Homemade cookies

Früchtebrot – glazed fruit cake

Chocolate tree decoration

Weihnachten

"This is how I write Christmas in German. Christmas is to celebrate the birth of Jesus Christ. His mother was called Mary, just like me! I have written a letter to Christkind, and I will leave it in the sitting room. This year, our Christmas tree is a really nice one. Last year we had a very prickly tree, but this one keeps all its needles."

ADVENT CALENDAR
Advent is the beginning of the church's year. It lasts from the end of November until 25 December. Maria has an advent calendar and each day she opens one of the numbered bags to find a treat.

Maria and Anna used shiny paper and string to make the heart decorations for their tree.

CHRISTMAS MARKET
A special feature of Advent is the enormous Christmas market at Stuttgart. It sells Christmas trees, decorations, and festive foods.

DECORATIVE TREE
The tradition of having a Christmas tree began in Germany in the Middle Ages. An evergreen tree was used as a symbol of everlasting life. People often decorate their trees with stars and angels as reminders of the Christmas story.

Star cookies

Straw angel

Bell for tree

This star is Maria's favourite decoration.

GIVING GIFTS
People give presents at Christmas to remind them of the gifts that the shepherds and the Wise Men took to the stable for Jesus. Maria's family buy gifts for each other, but the children's main gifts come from Christkind.

Anna waited until Maria was out to wrap the calendar that she had bought her for Christmas.

Maria wrote a letter to Christkind on her computer. She asked him for a cassette recorder and told him she had been a good girl.

Wunschzettel

PRESENTS FROM CHRISTKIND
While Maria and Anna are at church on Christmas Eve, they believe that Christkind visits their home and delivers presents. The sisters can hardly wait to get back from church and open the beautifully giftwrapped parcels.

Epiphany

LIKE MANY OTHER SPANISH CHILDREN, eleven-year-old Alejandra from Madrid only opens some of her presents at Christmas. She is given the rest at Epiphany, or Three Kings' Day, which falls on 6 January. On the eve of this Christian festival, the children of Spain believe that the Three Kings, or Wise Men, who brought gifts to baby Jesus will also bring presents for them. In Madrid, there is a flamboyant procession through the streets, with the Three Kings throwing sweets to crowds of children who line the pavements.

"I give my letter to one of the Kings' pages. The pages stand in shopping centres."

BUYING *ROSCON* CAKE
The traditional twelfth night cake is called *roscón*, which means "ring-shaped roll". Alejandra and her family buy the sweet doughy cake from their local bakery on the morning of Epiphany.

The *roscón* cake can be filled with cream or chocolate and contains a lucky gift.

This toy house was the lucky gift in Alejandra's *roscón* cake.

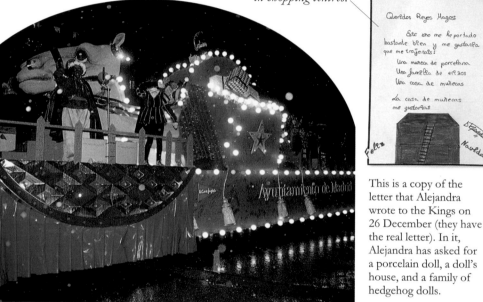

This is a copy of the letter that Alejandra wrote to the Kings on 26 December (they have the real letter). In it, Alejandra has asked for a porcelain doll, a doll's house, and a family of hedgehog dolls.

MELCHIOR'S FLOAT
Melchior has a long white beard and his chariot follows Gaspar's in the parade. Melchior gave Jesus gold. Gold is associated with kings and to Christians, Jesus is the King of Kings. In addition to the Kings' camel-shaped floats, there are also real camels in the parade. They follow the floats, carrying presents on their backs.

Gold

BALTHAZAR'S FLOAT
Alejandra's favourite King is Balthazar. Unlike the two other Kings, Balthazar has no beard. His chariot is last in the procession, and is in the shape of a gigantic camel — so big in fact that Alejandra could barely see Balthazar! Balthazar is said to have given baby Jesus a perfume called myrrh, which is put on dead bodies. This was meant to show that Jesus would suffer and die.

Myrrh

GASPAR'S FLOAT
Gaspar is easily recognized by his brown beard and brown hair. Dressed in a green cloak with an opulent green bejewelled crown, he leads the procession of the Three Kings. Gaspar gave Jesus a spice called frankincense, which is used in worship. This showed that people would worship Jesus.

Frankincense

ALEJANDRA'S NATIVITY
Many Nativity scenes show the shepherds and the Wise Men or Kings visiting baby Jesus at the same time. However, according to the Bible, the two events happened separately. The kings arrived at the stable on 6 January, a date known to most Christians as Epiphany. The Spanish word for nativity is *nacimientos*.

"The roscón is tasty, but I don't like the coloured fruit on top."

Fiesta de los tres Reyes Magos

Alejandra made this clay model of Joseph, Mary, and baby Jesus.

"This is how I write the Festival of the Three Magic Kings in Spanish. I wrote my letter to the Kings on 26 December, and then on the morning of 6 January, I woke up at 7 o'clock. I went straight to the Christmas tree, and saw that the Kings had been. The presents were there and two of the glasses of cognac were empty. I don't think Balthazar drank his, because he doesn't drink alcohol."

"We put our shoes under the Christmas tree, but the Kings leave most of our presents around the room."

"On my tray, I have the Three Kings made of chocolate. I can't wait to eat them!'

"The Kings left a Hunchback of Notre Dame music cassette in my shoe."

Alejandra's shoes

KING'S SNACKS
When she gets back from the procession, Alejandra puts out a pair of her shoes for the Kings to fill with presents. To give them strength for a long, cold night of delivering gifts, Alejandra leaves each of the Kings a glass of cognac, a satsuma, and some walnuts, as well as a bucket of water for the camels that bring them.

Bag of coal

CARBON

Walnuts

When Spanish children are naughty, the Kings leave them pieces of coal made of sugar among their presents.

Satsumas

"I didn't get any coal this year because I was good. I got some last year, but I didn't mind because it is sweet and I could eat it."

Alejandra's Epiphany presents

"I asked the Kings for hedgehogs but I got bears instead."

Our travels

"FOR A YEAR, Barnabas and I travelled to 18 different countries with British Airways, following the world's most famous festivals. From the flamboyant Carnival in Rio de Janeiro, to the N'cwala harvest festival in Zambia, we made many special friends along the way. They showed us their favourite festivals, and gave us festive foods to try. The only drawback was the amount of camera equipment we had to carry. It weighed 110 kgs in total, which is both of our weights put together!"

We made this book with UNICEF. They introduced us to many of the children we photographed, like M'sangombe in Zambia. UNICEF also drove the children to our studio in their special truck.

To get him to relax and enjoy the photography, Barnabas taught Pratab how to photograph his favourite Holi colour.

We keep the film inside this brown bag. We used 400 rolls of film for this book.

Sometimes we only had a tiny space in which to set up our studio. It was a squash for Raksha Bandhan because all the children at Suman and Manoj's school wanted to watch the photography.

This carton contains a roll of paper that we use as a background for photographing small items like food.

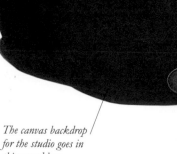

At other times, there wasn't a room big enough to set up our studio and Barnabas had to do the photography outside. He had a difficult time photographing Sonu for Diwali because the *diye* (clay lamps) kept blowing out in the wind.

The canvas backdrop for the studio goes in this round bag.

UNICEF gave us these stickers for our bags. In many countries, people helped us because we were working with UNICEF and UNICEF has helped them in many ways.

In Zambia, we saw some of the fabulous work that UNICEF is doing to assist children.

Getting to know each child was my favourite part of making *Celebration!*. Through a translator, Diego from Mexico chatted to me for a long time about "Day of the Dead".

During Esala Perahera in Sri Lanka, it rained so heavily that Barnabas had to strap an umbrella to himself, to stop his cameras getting wet.

Barnabas stood on top of a UNICEF vehicle so that he could see the N'cwala ceremony over the crowds.

In this little black bag is my computer for writing the book, and valuables, such as travellers cheques, foreign currency, passports, and tickets.

Pratab and Padmini completely covered Barnabas in red powder paint at the festival of Holi in India.

The tripods for holding up the canvas backdrop are in this long bag.

The tripods for the lights are kept in here.

The children at the N'cwala taught me the names of the Ngoni people's costume.

This is our suitcase. We pack clothes for hot and cold countries, a first aid kit, a tape recorder for interviewing, and presents for the children. That's about all we can fit in!

This hard black case contains all of Barnabas's cameras. There are three cameras and nine different lenses for photographing near and distant objects.

This is one of the heaviest cases. It holds the battery pack, which powers the lights.

All the lights go inside these two black cases. The cases are waterproof, to protect their valuable contents.

At Chinese New Year, I got cuddles from Man Po and her little sister, Hei Po.

Celebration! calendar

Festivals are special occasions that offer people the chance to celebrate together. Some of the main ones are listed here.

Tangerines from Hong Kong

Red and yellow Holi powders from India

M'sangombe celebrates the harvest festival of N'cwala in Zambia in February.

JANUARY

1 • New Year's Day
6 • Epiphany, Festival of the Three Magic Kings *Christian*
12, 13 • Lohri *Hindu*
13, 14 • Makar Sankranti *Hindu*
15, 16 • Pongal *Hindu*
15 • Martin Luther King Day, US
26 • Republic Day, India
26 • Australia Day

Firecrackers from Hong Kong

FEBRUARY

2 • Candlemas *Christian*
3 • Setsubun, Japan
6 • Waitangi Day, New Zealand
11 • National Foundation Day, Japan
15 • Nehar *Jewish*

MOVEABLE DATES
Argungu Fishing Festival, Nigeria
Shrove Tuesday *Christian*
Carnival *Christian*
Mardi Gras *Christian*
N'cwala Harvest Festival, Zambia

MARCH

1 • St. David's Day, Wales
3 • Hina Matsuri, Japan
6 • National Day, Ghana
17 • St. Patrick's Day, Ireland
23 • National Day, Pakistan
25 • National Day, Greece

MOVEABLE DATES
Hola Mohalla *Sikh*
Holi *Hindu*
Purim *Jewish*

Krishna, the Hindu god associated with Holi.

JANUARY–FEBRUARY
Tu B'Shevat *Jewish*
Shab e-Barat *Muslim*
Basant Panchami *Hindu*
Chinese New Year

FEBRUARY–MARCH
Maghapuja *Buddhist*
Shivratri *Hindu*

MARCH–APRIL
Mother's Day *Christian*
Easter *Christian*

Each March, Sayo takes part in the Japanese festival of Hina Matsuri.

Matilde's roses for Fête des Mères

Guava

JULY

1 • National Day, Canada
4 • US Independence Day
9 • National Day, Argentina
14 • Bastille Day, France
21 • National Day, Belgium

AUGUST

1 • National Day, Switzerland
6 • National Day, Bolivia
17 • National Day, Indonesia

MOVEABLE DATES
Esala Perahera *Buddhist*
Raksha Bandhan, India
Eisteddfod Day, Wales

Buddha

SEPTEMBER

7 • National Day, Brazil
16 • National Day, Mexico
18 • National Day, Chile
30 • National Day, Botswana

MOVEABLE DATES
Rosh Hashanah *Jewish*

Moon cake from Vietnam

These pom poms are called *savaran.*

JULY–AUGUST
O Bon, Family Remembrance Day, Japan
Tish B'Av *Jewish*

AUGUST–SEPTEMBER
Janamashtmi *Hindu*
Onam *Hindu*
Ganesh Chaturthi *Hindu*

SEPTEMBER–OCTOBER
Yom Kippur *Jewish*
Succot *Jewish*
Trung Thu, Vietnam

Ajit is a *savaran*, or pom pom, dancer in the Buddhist festival of Esala Perahera, which takes place each year in Sri Lanka.

Pineapple from Sri Lanka

ISLAMIC FESTIVALS
There are no fixed dates for Islamic festivals because every year, each Islamic month begins 11 days earlier than the previous year.

Eid ul-Fitr • Ramadan • Eid ul-Adha
Birthday of the Prophet Mohammad
Lailat ul-Qadr

Suman puts a holy mark called a *tilak* on Manoj's forehead.

Brothers and sisters, like Manoj and Suman, show their love for each other every August in the Indian festival of Raksha Bandhan.

Vân's moon cake is called *bánh Nuong.*

Each autumn, Vân celebrates Trung Thu, the Vietnamese moon festival.

Kazu celebrates Kodomono-hi (Children's Day) in Japan in May.

Sophie decorated the story of her May Day with drawings of spring flowers.

Spring flowers from England

THE FESTIVAL CALENDAR

Many festivals, such as national holidays, take place on the same day each year. Religious festivals are often based on the appearance of the moon or on ancient religious calendars and therefore take place at different times throughout the year.

APRIL

4, 5 • Ch'ing Ming Festival, Hong Kong
13, 14 • Baisakhi *Sikh*
14, 15 • Vishu *Hindu*
21 • First Day of Ridvan *Baha'i*
23 • Egemenlik Bayrami, Turkey
23 • St. George's Day, England
29 • Ninth Day of Ridvan *Baha'i*

MOVEABLE DATES
Passover *Jewish*
Ram Navami *Hindu*

MAY

Carp kite from Japan

1 • May Day, northern Europe
2 • Twelfth Day of Ridvan *Baha'i*
3 • National Day, Poland
5 • Kodomono-hi, Japan
17 • National Day, Norway
23 • Declaration of the Bab *Baha'i*
28, 29 • Ascension of Baha'u'llah *Baha'i*

MOVEABLE DATES
Ascension Day *Christian*
Cheung Cha Bun Festival, Hong Kong
Fête des Mères *Christian*

JUNE

2 • Republic Day, Italy
6 • National Day, Sweden
12 • Russian Independence Day
23 • Midsummer's Eve

MOVEABLE DATES
Corpus Christi *Christian*
Dragon Boat Festival, China

Sophie celebrates May Day in England at the beginning of May.

APRIL–MAY
Lag B'Omer *Jewish*

MAY–JUNE
Shavout *Jewish*
Visakhapuja *Buddhist*
Pentecost *Christian*

JUNE–JULY

St. Lucia crown, Sweden

Christmas cookies

OCTOBER

1 • National Day, China
9 • National Day, Uganda
12 • National Day, Spain
12 • Columbus Day
24 • United Nations Day
24 • National Day, Zambia
26 • National Day, Austria
31 • Hallowe'en

MOVEABLE DATES
Dussehra *Hindu*
Simhat Torah *Jewish*
Thanksgiving (2nd Monday in October), Canada

Sugar skull from Mexico

NOVEMBER

1 • All Saints' Day *Christian*
2 • All Souls' Day *Christian*
1, 2 • Day of the Dead *Christian*
5 • Guy Fawkes Day, UK
30 • St. Andrew's Day, Scotland

Thanksgiving (4th Thursday in November), United States

Diya from India

DECEMBER

6 • National Day, Finland
6 • St. Nicholas' Day *Christian*
9 • National Day, Tanzania
12 • National Day, Kenya
13 • St. Lucia's Day *Christian*
24 • Christmas Eve *Christian*
25 • Christmas Day *Christian*
26 • St. Stephen's Day
26 • Boxing Day
31 • New Year's Eve

MOVEABLE DATES
Hanukkah *Jewish*
Kwanzaa (African-American harvest festival)

OCTOBER–NOVEMBER
Diwali *Hindu/Sikh*
Guru Nanak's birthday *Sikh*

NOVEMBER–DECEMBER

DECEMBER–JANUARY

Isabel celebrates the Jewish festival of Hanukkah in December.

Isabel is holding her family candlestick, or *hanukkiya*.

Maria and her sister love singing carols to celebrate the Christian festival of Christmas in December.

Maria's favourite carol is "Silent Night".

Karin celebrates St. Lucia's Day, the Swedish festival of light, in December.

Festive cookies decorate the Christmas tree in Maria's home.

Index

Acknowledgments

Barnabas and Anabel would like to thank:
All the children and their parents who participated in the book; our special team of Fiona Robertson and Rebecca Johns, Rachel Beaugie; Robert Smith at UNICEF UK Committee; Priscilla and James Chow; Tim Chung; Mrs Haynes at Northill Primary School; Theo Thomas; Joseph M. Mahase, Anoja Wijesekera at UNICEF Sri Lanka; Mr Beddewela, Farahab Rahman, Helga and all at The Chalet; Swamy Saraswathy; Uncle, Aunty, and Mythili; Sunisha at Mobile Crèches; Bikram Grewal; Rima Salah, Rodney Hatfield, Mr Nguyen Tinh, Dr Tinh, Sandy Blanchet at UNICEF, Hanoi; Beth Berton-Hunter, Barbara Strang at UNICEF, Ontario; Vicky Dorosch, Sue Chaiton, Suzanne Hollsworth of Fenn Publishing, Rafáel Enriquez at UNICEF, Mexico; Miguel A. Nuñez; Maurizio and Juana Dolores; Ranjit Singh; Allison Devlin, Julia Beck, Nancy Lieberman at

DK Inc.; Peter and Maria Hroziencik; Magdalena Fazekasova at Perfekt; Sandra Nováková, Bratislava; Camilla Andersson at UNICEF National Committee, Sweden; Elisabeth Brundin at Nordic Museum, Stockholm; Käppala Skola, Sweden; Irmagard Schmatz at SDK; Soledad and Marga Arthurs at UNICEF, Madrid, Sylvie and Jacques and the children; Katherine Kindersley; Angela Alvarez Matheus at UNICEF, Rio, Martha Lima, Angela Melim; Nancy Lo at UNICEF, Hong Kong; Jalal al Azzeh at UNICEF, Jordan, Issam and Fatimah Mihyar; Mark Stirling, Claire Blenkinsop, Zarina Geloo, Damiano at UNICEF, Zambia; Akihiko Morita, Yumiko Aoki at UNICEF National Committee, Tokyo and Osaka; Praamit Chanda (DKFL, India), Prithvi Singh and his family, Jaipur; Richard and Fatima Reid, Alanor Olali at UNICEF National Committee, Turkey, Göver Sünerin, Necdet Kaygin; Maria Chordi and

family, Richard Pankhurst, Konjit Seyoum, Alula Pankhurst; Clive; all the children that bought our last book, enabling us to make this one!

Dorling Kindersley would also like to thank:
Ann Cannings and Maggie Tingle for additional design assistance; Rachel Beaugie and Nichola Roberts for additional editorial assistance; Chris Bernstein for the index; Vicky Haeri and Tina Omari at UNICEF in New York; Stuart Booy at STA Travel; Jacky Ive and Mary Brew at British Airways.
Additional photographs
Key: l = left, r = right, t = top, b = bottom, a = above, c = centre
The publisher would like to thank the following for their kind permission to reproduce the photographs
Faith Eaton: 31cr; **Robert Harding Picture Library:** Dave Reede 40 41; **David Richardson** 33ca; **Illustration Karl Stehle © by Art Color Verlag ®; Tony Stone Images:** John Starr 11br, Nabeel Turner 36cr; **Zefa:** L. Dantaus 10tl